T0206902

Computer Vision Using Deep Learning

Neural Network Architectures with Python and Keras

Vaibhav Verdhan

Apress®

Computer Vision Using Deep Learning: Neural Network Architectures with Python and Keras

Vaibhav Verdhan
Limerick, Ireland

ISBN-13 (pbk): 978-1-4842-6615-1   ISBN-13 (electronic): 978-1-4842-6616-8
https://doi.org/10.1007/978-1-4842-6616-8

Managing Director, Apress Media LLC: Welmoed Spahr
Acquisitions Editor: Aaron Black
Development Editor: James Markham
Coordinating Editor: Jessica Vakili

Distributed to the book trade worldwide by Springer Science+Business Media New York, 1 NY Plazar, New York, NY 10014. Phone 1-800-SPRINGER, fax (201) 348-4505, e-mail orders-ny@springer-sbm.com, or visit www.springeronline.com. Apress Media, LLC is a California LLC and the sole member (owner) is Springer Science + Business Media Finance Inc (SSBM Finance Inc). SSBM Finance Inc is a **Delaware** corporation.

For information on translations, please e-mail booktranslations@springernature.com; for reprint, paperback, or audio rights, please e-mail bookpermissions@springernature.com.

Apress titles may be purchased in bulk for academic, corporate, or promotional use. eBook versions and licenses are also available for most titles. For more information, reference our Print and eBook Bulk Sales web page at http://www.apress.com/bulk-sales.

Any source code or other supplementary material referenced by the author in this book is available to readers on GitHub via the book's product page, located at www.apress.com/978-1-4842-6615-1. For more detailed information, please visit http://www.apress.com/source-code.

Printed on acid-free paper

To Yashi, Pakhi and Rudra

Table of Contents

About the Author

Vaibhav Verdhan is a seasoned data science professional with rich experience spanning across geographies and domains. He is a hands-on technical expert and has led multiple engagements in machine learning and artificial intelligence. He is a leading industry expert, is a regular speaker at conferences and meetups, and mentors students and professionals. Currently, he resides in Ireland and is working as a Principal Data Scientist.

About the Technical Reviewer

Vishwesh Ravi Shrimali graduated from BITS Pilani in 2018, where he studied mechanical engineering. Since then, he has worked with Big Vision LLC on Deep Learning and computer vision and was involved in creating official OpenCV AI courses. Currently, he is working at Mercedes-Benz Research and Development India Pvt. Ltd. He has a keen interest in programming and AI and has applied that interest in mechanical engineering projects. He has also written multiple blogs on OpenCV and Deep Learning on Learn OpenCV, a leading blog on computer vision. He has also coauthored *Machine learning for OpenCV 4* (second edition) by Packt. When he is not writing blogs or working on projects, he likes to go on long walks or play his acoustic guitar.

Acknowledgments

I would like to express my thanks to the following people. It is the results of their hard work and passion that are advancing this field:

Ross Girshick

Jeff Donahue

Trevor Darrell

Jitendra Malik

Shaoqing Ren

Kaiming He

Jian Sun

Christian Szegedy

Wei Liu

Yangqing Jia

Pierre Sermanet

Scott Reed

Dragomir Anguelov

Dumitru Erhan

Vincent Vanhoucke

Andrew Rabinovich

Sergey Ioffe

Jonathon Shlens

Xiangyu Zhang

Omkar M. Parkhi

Andrea Vedaldi

Andrew Zisserman

Yaniv Taigman

Ming Yang

ACKNOWLEDGMENTS

Marc'Aurelio Ranzato

Lior Wolf

Yann LeCun

Leon Bottou

Yoshua Bengio

Patrick Haffner

Sefik Ilkin Serengil

Introduction

Innovation distinguishes between a leader and a follower.

—Steve Jobs

How good is your driving? Will you drive better than an autonomous driving system? Or do you think an algorithm will perform better than a specialist in classifying medical images? It can be a tricky question. But artificial intelligence has outperformed doctors in detecting lung cancer and breast cancer by analyzing images! Ouch!

Nature has been very kind to grant us powers of sight, taste, smell, touch, and hearing. Out of these senses, the power of sight allows us to appreciate the beauty of the world, enjoy the colors, recognize the faces of our family and loved ones, and above all relish this beautiful world and life. With time, humans amplified the power of the brain and made path-breaking inventions and discoveries. The wheel or airplane, printing press or clock, light bulb or personal computers – innovations have changed the way we live, work, travel, decide, and progress. These innovations make life simpler, easier, and far enjoyable and safe.

Data science and Deep Learning are allowing us to further enhance the innovative buckets. Using Deep Learning, we are able to replicate the power of vision given by nature. The computers are being trained to perform the same tasks done by a human being. It can be detection of colors or shape or size, classifying between a cat or a dog or a horse, or driving on a road – the use cases are many. The solutions are applicable for all the sectors like retail, manufacturing, BFSI, agriculture, security, transport, pharmaceuticals, and so on.

This book is an attempt to explain the concepts of Deep Learning and Neural Network for computer vision problems. We are examining convolutional Neural Networks in detail, and their various components and attributes. We are exploring various Neural Network architectures like LeNet, AlexNet, VGG, R-CNN, Fast R-CNN, Faster R-CNN, SSD, YOLO, ResNet, Inception, DeepFace, and FaceNet in detail. We are also developing pragmatic solutions to tackle use cases of binary image classification, multiclass image classification, object detection, face recognition, and video analytics. We will use Python and Keras for the solutions. All the codes and datasets are checked into the GitHub repo for quick access. In the final chapter, we are studying all the steps in a Deep Learning project – right from defining the business problem to deployment. We are also dealing with major errors and issues faced while developing the solutions. Throughout the book, we are providing tips and tricks for training better algorithms, reducing the training time, monitoring the results, and improving the solution. We are also sharing prominent research papers and datasets which you should use to gain further knowledge.

The book is suitable for researchers and students who want to explore and implement computer vision solutions using Deep Learning. It is highly useful and hence recommended for professionals who intend to explore cutting-edge technology, grasp the advanced concepts, develop a thorough understanding of Deep Learning architectures, and get the best practices and solutions to common computer vision challenges. It is directed toward the business leaders who wish to implement Deep Learning solutions in their business and gain confidence while they communicate with their teams and clientele. Above all, for a curious person trying to explore how Deep Learning algorithms work for solving computer vision problems and would like to try Python.

I would like to thank Apress, Aaron, Jessica, and Vishwesh for believing in me and giving me the chance to work on this subject. And a special word of thanks to my family – Yashi, Pakhi, and Rudra – for the excellent support without which it would be impossible to complete this work.

Vaibhav Verdhan, November 2020, Limerick

Foreword

Computer Vision, not too long ago the exclusive purview of science fiction, is quickly becoming commonplace across industries, if not in society at large. The progress in the field to emulate human vision, that most prized of human senses, is nothing but astonishing. It was only 1957 when Russell Kirsch scanned the world's first photograph, a black and white image of his boy[1]. By the late 1980s, the work of Sirovich and Kirby[2] helped establish face recognition as a viable technology for biometric applications. Facebook made the technology ubiquitous, notwithstanding privacy concerns and legal challenges action[3], when in 2010, it incorporated face recognition in its social media platform.

The capabilities of Deep Learning vision systems to interpret and extract information from images permeates all aspects of society. Only the most skeptical among us doubt a not too distant future with self-driving cars outnumbering those driven by their human counterparts or computer-aided diagnosis (CADx) of medical images becoming an ordinary service supplied by medical providers. Computer vision applications

---

[1]The Associated Press "Computer scientist, pixel inventor Russell Kirsch dead at 91", *The Associated Press*, AP News, August 13, 2020, https://apnews.com/article/technology-oregon-science-portland-us-news-db92e0b593f5156da970c0a1e9f90944. Accessed 9 December 2020.

[2]Low-Dimensional Procedure for the Characterization of Human Faces, L. Sirovich and M Kirby, March 1987, Journal of the Optical Society of America. A, Optics and image science 4(3):519-24

[3]Natasha Singer and Mike Isaac "Facebook to Pay $550 Million to Settle Facial Recognition Suit" *The New York Times*, Jan 29, 2020 , https://www.nytimes.com/2020/01/29/technology/facebook-privacy-lawsuit-earnings.html. Accessed 9 December 2020.

already control access to our mobile devices and can outperform human inspectors in the tedious but critical task of inspecting for defects in all types of manufacturing processes. That is how I met Vaibhav, or V, as he is known to his friends and colleagues. Collaborating on methods to improve existing computer vision systems to ensure defect-free products critical for human vision. Not lost is an appreciation of the circular history. We teach computers how to see; they help manufacture products vital to improve and care for human vision.

In this book, V takes a practical and convenient approach to the subject. The abundant use of case studies is facilitated by ready-to-use Python code and links to datasets and other tools. The practitioner's learning experience is enhanced by access to the resources needed to work in a step-by-step fashion through each case study. The book organizes the subject into three parts. In chapters 1 through 4, V describes the nature of Neural Networks and demystifies how they learn. Along the way, he points out different architectures and their historical significance. The practitioner gets to experience, with all required resources in hand, the elegant simplicity of LeNet, the improved efficiency of AlexNet, and the popular VGG Net. In chapters 5 through 7, the practitioner applies simple yet powerful computer vision applications such as training systems to detect objects and recognize human faces. When progressing into performing video analytics, we encounter the nagging problem of vanishing and exploding gradients and how to overcome it using skip connections in the ResNet architecture. Finally, in chapter 8, we review the complete model development process, starting with a correctly defined business problem and systematically advancing until the model is deployed and maintain in a production environment.

We are now just starting to see the dramatic increase in complexity and impact of tasks performed by computer systems that match and often exceed what until recently, would be considered exclusively human vision capabilities. Those aspiring to make this technology their ally, grow more adept at incorporating vision systems into their practice, and become a more skillful practitioner will greatly gain from the tools, techniques, and methods presented in this book.

David O. Ramos

Jacksonville, FL

16 December 2020

CHAPTER 1

Introduction to Computer Vision and Deep Learning

Vision is the best gift to mankind by God.

Right from our birth, vision allows us to develop a conscious mind. Colors, shapes, objects, and faces are all building blocks for our world. This gift of nature is quite central to our senses.

Computer vision is one of the capabilities which allows the machines to replicate this power. And using Deep Learning, we are enhancing our command and making advancements in this field.

This book will examine the concepts of computer vision in the light of Deep Learning. We will study the basic building blocks of Neural Networks, develop pragmatic use cases by taking a case study–based approach, and compare and contrast the performance of various solutions. We will discuss the best practices, share the tips and insights followed in the industry, make you aware of the common pitfalls, and develop a thought process to design Neural Networks.

© Vaibhav Verdhan 2021
V. Verdhan, *Computer Vision Using Deep Learning*,
https://doi.org/10.1007/978-1-4842-6616-8_1

Throughout the book, we introduce a concept, explore it in detail, and then develop a use case in Python around it. Since a chapter first builds the foundations of Deep Learning and then its pragmatic usage, the complete knowledge enables you to design a solution and then develop Neural Networks for better decision making.

Some knowledge of Python and object-oriented programming concepts is expected for a good understanding. A basic to intermediate understanding of data science is advisable though not a necessary requirement.

In this introductory chapter, we will develop the concepts of Image Processing using OpenCV and Deep Learning. OpenCV is a great library and is widely used in robotics, face recognition, gesture recognition, AR, and so on. Deep Learning, in addition, offers a higher level of complexity and flexibility to develop Image Processing use cases. We will cover the following topics in this chapter:

(1)   Image Processing using OpenCV

(2)   Fundamentals of Deep Learning

(3)   How Deep Learning works

(4)   Popular Deep Learning libraries

1.1 Technical requirements

We are developing all the solutions in Python throughout the book; hence, installation of the latest version of Python is required.

All the code, datasets, and respective results are checked into a code repository at `https://github.com/Apress/computer-vision-using-deep-learning/tree/main/Chapter1`. You are advised to run all the code with us and replicate the results. This will strengthen your grasp on the concepts.

1.2 Image Processing using OpenCV

An image is also like any other data point. On our computers and mobile phones, it appears as an object or icon in .jpeg, .bmp, and .png formats. Hence, it becomes difficult for humans to visualize it in a row-column structure, like we visualize any other database. Hence, it is often referred to as *unstructured data*.

For our computers and algorithms to analyze an image and work on it, we have to represent an image in the form of integers. Hence, we work on an image pixel by pixel. Mathematically, one of the ways to represent each pixel is the RGB (Red, Green, Blue) value. We use this information to do the Image Processing.

Info   The easiest way to get RGB for any color is to open it in Paint in Windows operating system. Hover over any color and get the respective RGB value. In Mac OS, you can use Digital Colour Meter.

Deep Learning allows us to develop use cases which are much more complex to be resolved using traditional Image Processing techniques. For example, detecting a face can be done using OpenCV too, but to be able to recognize one will require Deep Learning.

During the process of developing computer vision solutions using Deep Learning, we prepare our image dataset first. During preparation, we might have to perform grayscaling of the images, detect contours, crop the images, and then feed them to the Neural Network.

OpenCV is the most famous library for such tasks. As a first step, let's develop some building blocks of these Image Processing methods. We will create three solutions using OpenCV.

Note   Go to www.opencv.org and follow the instructions over there to get OpenCV installed on your system.

The images used for the solutions are the commonly available ones. You are advised to examine the code and follow the step-by-step implementation done. We will detect shape, colors, and a face in an image.

Let's dive into the exciting world of images!

1.2.1 Color detection using OpenCV

When we think of an image, it is made up of shapes, sizes, and colors. Having the capability to detect shape, size, or color in an image can automate a lot of processes and save huge efforts. In the very first example, we are going to develop a "color detection system."

Color detection is having a wide range of utility across domains and industries like manufacturing, automotive, electricity, utilities, and so on. Color detection can be used to look for abruptions, failures, and disruptions to normal behavior. We can train sensors to take a particular decision based on the color and raise an alarm if required.

An image is represented using pixels, and each pixel is made up of RGB values ranging from 0 to 255. We will be using this property to identify the blue color in the image (Figure 1-1). You can change the respective values for the blue color and detect any color of choice.

Follow these steps:

1. Open the Python Jupyter Notebook.

2. First load the necessary libraries, numpy and OpenCV.

    ```
    import numpy as np
    import cv2
    ```

3. Load the image file.

    ```
    image = cv2.imread('Color.png')
    ```

Figure 1-1. *Raw image to be used for color detection. The image shown has four different colors, and the OpenCV solution will detect them individually*

4. Now let us convert our raw image to HSV (Hue Saturation Value) format. It enables us to separate from saturation and pseudo-illumination. cv2.cvtColor allows us to do that.

```
hsv_convert = cv2.cvtColor(image, cv2.COLOR_BGR2HSV)
```

5. Define the upper and lower ranges of the color here. We are detecting the blue color. From the numpy library, we have given the respective range for the blue color.

```
lower_range = np.array([110,50,50])
upper_range = np.array([130,255,255])
```

6. Now, let's detect the blue color and separate it from the rest of the image.

```
mask_toput = cv2.inRange(hsv_convert, lower_range,
upper_range)
cv2.imshow('image', image)
cv2.imshow('mask', mask_toput)
while(True):
k = cv2.waitKey(5)& 0xFF if k== 27: break
```

The output of this code will be as shown in Figure 1-2.

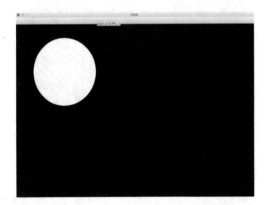

Figure 1-2. *Output of the colour detection system. We want to detect blue colour which is detected and separated from rest of the image*

As visible, the blue color is highlighted in white, while the rest of the image is in black. By changing the ranges in step 5, you can detect different colors of your choice.

With color done, it is time to detect a shape in an image; let's do it!

1.3 Shape detection using OpenCV

Like we detected the blue color in the last section, we will detect triangle, square, rectangle, and circle in an image. Shape detection allows you to separate portions in the image and check for patterns. Color and shape detections make a solution very concrete. The usability lies in safety monitoring, manufacturing lines, automobile centers, and so on.

For Shape detection, we get the contours of each shape, check the number of elements, and then classify accordingly. For example, if this number is three, it is a triangle. In this solution, you will also observe how to grayscale an image and detect contours.

Follow these steps to detect shapes:

1. Import the libraries first.

```
import numpy as np
import cv2
```

2. Load the raw image now shown in Figure 1-3.

```
shape_image = cv2.imread('shape.png')
```

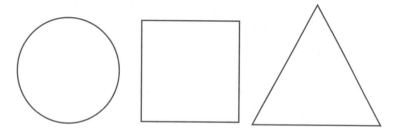

Figure 1-3. *Raw input image for detecting the three shapes of circle, triangle, and rectangle*

3. Convert the image to grayscale next. Grayscaling is done for simplicity since RGB is three-dimensional while grayscale is two-dimensional, and converting to grayscale simplifies the solution. It also makes the code efficient.

```
gray_image = cv2.cvtColor(shape_image, cv2.COLOR_BGR2GRAY)
ret,thresh = cv2.threshold(gray_image,127,255,1)
```

4. Find the contours in the image.

```
contours,h = cv2.findContours(thresh,1,2)
```

5. Try to approximate each of the contours using
    approxPolyDP. This method returns the number of
    elements in the contours detected. Then we decide the
    shape based on the number of elements in the contours.
    If the value is three, it is a triangle; if it's four, it is a
    square; and so on.

```
for cnt in contours:
    approx =
    cv2.approxPolyDP(cnt,0.01*cv2.arcLength(cnt,True),True)
print (len(approx))
if len(approx)==3:
    print ("triangle")
    cv2.drawContours(shape_image,[cnt],0,(0,255,0),-1)
elif len(approx)==4:
    print ("square")
    cv2.drawContours(shape_image,[cnt],0,(0,0,255),-1)
elif len(approx) > 15:
    print ("circle")
    cv2.drawContours(shape_image,[cnt],0,(0,255,255),-1)
cv2.imshow('shape_image',shape_image)    cv2.waitKey(0)
cv2.destroyAllWindows()
```

6. The output of the preceding code is shown in Figure 1-4.

Figure 1-4. *The output of the color detection system. A circle is shown
in yellow, square is shown in red, and triangle is shown in green*

You can now detect shapes in any image. We have detected a circle, a triangle, and a square. A good challenge will be to detect a pentagon or hexagon; are you game?

Let's do something more fun now!

1.3.1 Face detection using OpenCV

Face detection is not a new capability. Whenever we look at a picture, we can recognize a face quite easily. Our mobile phone camera draws square boxes around a face. Or on social media, a square box is created around a face. It is called *face detection.*

Face detection refers to locating human faces in digital images. Face detection is different from face recognition. In the former, we are only detecting a face in an image, whereas in the latter we are putting a name to the face too, that is, who is the person in the photo.

Most of the modern cameras and mobiles have a built-in capability to detect faces. A similar solution can be developed using OpenCV. It is simpler to understand and implement and is built using the Haar-cascade algorithm. We will highlight faces and eyes in a photograph while using this algorithm in Python.

Haar-cascade classifier is used to detect faces and other facial attributes like eyes in an image. It is a Machine Learning solution wherein training is done on a lot of images which have a face and which do not have a face in them. The classifier learns the respective features. Then we use the same classifier to detect faces for us. We need not do any training here as the classifier is already trained and ready to be used. Saves time and effort, too!

Info   Object detection using Haar-based cascade classifiers was proposed by Paul Viola and Michael Jones in their paper "Rapid Object Detection using a Boosted Cascade of Simple Features" in 2001. You are advised to go through this path-breaking paper.

Follow these steps to detect a face:

1. Import the libraries first.

    ```python
    import numpy as np
    import cv2
    ```

2. Load the classifier xml file. The .xml file is designed
    by OpenCV and is created by training cascade of
    negative faces superimposed on positive images and
    hence can detect the facial features.

    ```python
    face_cascade = cv2.CascadeClassifier(
    'haarcascade_frontalface_default.xml')
    eye_cascade = cv2.CascadeClassifier(
    'haarcascade_eye.xml')
    ```

3. Next, load the image (Figure 1-5).

    ```python
    img = cv2.imread('Vaibhav.jpg')
    ```

Figure 1-5. *Raw input image of a face which is used for the face
detection using the Haar-cascade solution*

4. Convert the image to grayscale.

    ```python
    gray = cv2.cvtColor(img, cv2.COLOR_BGR2GRAY)
    ```

5. Execute the following code to detect a face in the image. If any face is found, we return the position of the detected face as Rect(x,y,w,h). Subsequently, the eyes are detected on the face.

```
faces = face_cascade.detectMultiScale(gray, 1.3, 5)
for (x,y,w,h) in faces:
image = cv2.rectangle(image,(x,y),(x+w,y+h),
(255,0,0),2) roi_gr = gray[y:y+h, x:x+w]
roi_clr = img[y:y+h, x:x+w]
the_eyes = eye_cascade.detectMultiScale(roi_gr)
for (ex,ey,ew,eh) in the_eyes:
    cv2.rectangle(roi_clr,(ex,ey),(ex+ew,ey+eh),
    (0,255,0),2)
    cv2.imshow('img',image) cv2.waitKey(0)
    cv2.destroyAllWindows()
```

6. The output is shown in Figure 1-6. Have a look how a blue box is drawn around the face and two green small boxes are around the eyes.

Figure 1-6. *Face and eyes detected in the image; a green box is around the eyes and blue square around the face*

Face detection allows us to find faces in images and videos. It is the first step for face recognition. It is used widely for security applications, attendance monitoring, and so on. We will be developing face detection and recognition using Deep Learning in subsequent chapters.

We have studied some of the concepts of Image Processing. It is time to examine and learn the concepts of Deep Learning. These are the building blocks for the journey you have embarked upon.

1.4 Fundamentals of Deep Learning

Deep Learning is a subfield of Machine Learning. The "deep" in Deep Learning is having successive layers of representation; hence, the depth of the model refers to the number of layers in the Artificial Neural Network (ANN) model and is essentially referred to as Deep Learning.

It is a novel approach to analyze historical data and learn from successive layers of increasingly meaningful representations. The typical process in a Deep Learning project is similar to a Machine Learning project as described in the following and shown in Figure 1-7.

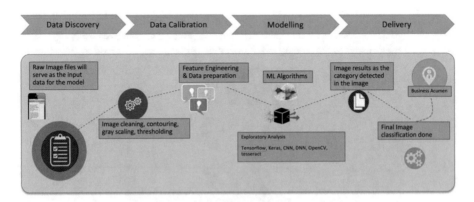

Figure 1-7. *End-to-end machine learning process from data discovery to the final development of the solution. All the steps are discussed in detail here and are again revisited in Chapter 8 of the book*

1. Data ingestion: Raw data files/image/text and so on are ingested into the system. They serve as the input data to train and test the network.

2. Data cleaning: In this step, we clean the data. Often, there is too much noise like junk values, duplicates, NULL, and outliers present in a structured dataset. All such data points have to be treated at this stage. For images, we might have to remove the unnecessary noise in the images.

3. Data preparation: We make our data ready for training. In this step, new derived variables might be required, or we might need to rotate/crop images in case we are working on image datasets.

4. Exploratory data analysis: We perform initial analysis to generate quick insights about our datasets.

5. Network design and training the model: We design our Neural Network here and decide on the number of hidden layers, nodes, activation functions, loss functions, and so on. The network is then trained.

6. Check the accuracy and iterate: We measure the accuracy of the network. We use the Confusion Matrix, AUC value, precision, recall, and so on to measure. Then we tune the hyperparameters and tune further.

7. The final model is presented to the business and we get the feedback.

8. We iterate the model and improve it based on the feedback received and a final solution is created.

9. The model is deployed to production. It is then maintained and refreshed at regular intervals.

These steps are typically followed during a Machine Learning project. We will be examining all these steps in great details in the last chapter of this book. It is now a good time to understand Neural Networks.

1.4.1 The motivation behind Neural Network

Artificial Neural Networks (ANNs) are said to be inspired by the way a human brain works. When we see a picture, we associate a label against it. We train our brain and senses to recognize a picture when we see it again and label it correctly.

ANN learns to perform similar tasks by learning or getting trained. This is done by looking at various examples of historical data points like transactional data or images and most of the time without being programmed for specific rules. For example, to distinguish between a car and a man, an ANN will start with no prior understanding and knowledge of the attributes of each of the class. It then generates attributes and the identification characteristics from the training data. It then learns those attributes and uses them later to make predictions.

Formally put, "learning" in the context of Artificial Neural Networks refers to adjusting the weights and the bias inside the network to improve the subsequent accuracy for the network. And an obvious way to do this is to reduce the error term which is nothing but the difference between the actual value and predicted value. To measure the error rate, we have a cost function defined which is rigorously evaluated during the learning phase of the network. We will be examining all these terms in detail in the next section.

A typical Neural Network looks like Figure 1-8.

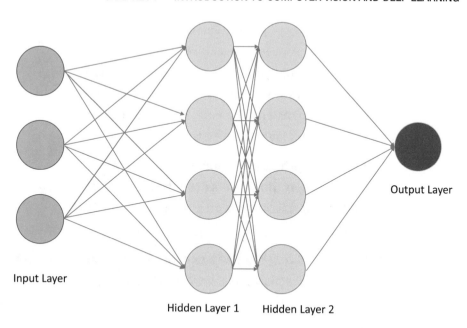

Figure 1-8. *A typical Neural Network with an input layer, hidden layers, and an output layer. Each layer has a few neurons inside it. Hidden layers act as the heart and soul of the network. The input layer accepts the input data, and the output layer is responsible for generating the final results*

The Neural Network shown earlier has three input units, two hidden layers with four neurons each, and one final output layer.

Now let us discuss various components of a Neural Network in subsequent sections.

1.4.2 Layers in a Neural Network

A basic Neural Network architecture consists of predominantly three layers:

- Input layer: As the name signifies, it receives the input data. Consider feeding raw images/processed images to the input layer. This is the first step of a Neural Network.

- Hidden layers: They are the heart and soul of the network. All the processing, feature extraction, learning, and training are done in these layers. Hidden layers break the raw data into attributes and features and learn the nuances of the data. This learning is used later in the output layer to make a decision.

- Output layer: The decision layer and final piece in a network. It accepts the outputs from the preceding hidden layers and then makes a judgment on the final classification.

The most granular building block of a network is a neuron. A neuron is where the entire magic takes place, which we are discussing next.

1.4.3 Neuron

A neuron or artificial neurons are the foundation of a Neural Network. The entire complex calculation takes place in a neuron only. A layer in the network can contain more than one neuron.

A neuron receives input from the previous layers or the input layers and then does the processing of the information and shares an output. The input data can be the raw data or processed information from a preceding neuron. The neuron then combines the input with their own internal state and reaches a value using an activation function (we'll discuss activation functions in a while). Subsequently, an output is generated using the output function.

A neuron can be thought of as Figure 1-9 where it receives the respective inputs and calculates the output.

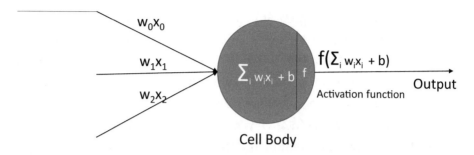

Figure 1-9. *A representation of a neuron receiving input from the previous layers and using the activation function to process and give the output. It is the building block of a Neural Network*

The input to a neuron is received from the output of its predecessors and their respective connections. The input received is calculated as a weighted sum, and a bias term is generally added too. This is the function of a *propagation function*. As shown in Figure 1-9, f is the activation function, w is the weight terms, and b is the bias term. After the calculations are done, we receive the output.

For example, the input training data will have raw images or processed images. These images will be fed to the input layer. The data now travels to the hidden layers where all the calculations are done. These calculations are done by neurons in each layer.

The output is the task that needs to be accomplished, for example, identification of an object or if we want to classify an image and so on.

Like we discussed, to a large extent, Neural Networks are able to extract the information themselves, but still we have to initiate a few parameters for the process of training the network. They are referred to as *hyperparameters* which we are discussing next.

1.4.4 Hyperparameters

During training a network, the algorithm is constantly learning the attributes of the raw data. But there are a few parameters which a network cannot learn itself and requires initial settings. Hyperparameters are those variables and attributes which an Artificial Neural Network cannot learn by itself. These are the variables that determine the structure of the Neural Network and the respective variables which are useful to train the network.

Hyperparameters are set before the actual training of the network. The learning rate, number of hidden layers in the network, number of neurons in each layer, activation function, number of epoch, batch size, dropout, and network weight initialization are examples of hyperparameters.

Tuning the hyperparameters is the process of choosing the best value for the hyperparameters based on its performance. We measure the performance of the network on the validation set and then tweak the hyperparameters and then reevaluate and retweak, and this process continues. We will examine various hyperparameters in the next section.

1.4.5 Connections and weight of ANN

The ANN consists of various connections. Each of the connections aims to receive the input and provide the computed output. This output serves as an input to the next neuron.

Also, each connection is assigned a weight which is a representative of its respective importance. It is important to note that a neuron can have multiple input and output connections which means it can receive inputs and deliver multiple signals.

The next term is again an important component – the bias term.

1.4.6 Bias term

Bias is just like adding an intercept value to a linear equation. It is an extra or additional parameter in a network.

The simplest way to understand bias is as per the following equation:

$$y = mx + c$$

If we do not have the constant term c, the equation will pass through (0,0). If we have the constant term c, we can expect a better fitting machine learning model.

As we can observe in Figure 1-10, on the left, we have a neuron without a bias term, while on the right we have added a bias term. So the bias allows us to adjust the output along with the weighted sum of the inputs.

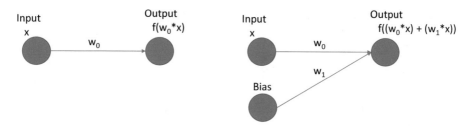

Figure 1-10. *A bias term helps in better fitting the model. On the left side, there is no bias term, and on the right we have the bias term. Note that the bias term has a weight associated with it*

The bias term hence acts like a constant term in a linear equation, and it helps in fitting the data better.

We will now study one of the most important attributes in a Neural Network – activation functions – in the next section.

1.4.7 Activation functions

The primary role of an activation function is to decide whether a neuron/perceptron should fire or not. They play a central role in adjusting the gradients during the training of the network at a later stage. An activation function is shown in Figure 1-9. They are sometimes referred to as *transfer functions.*

The nonlinear behavior of activation functions allows Deep Learning networks to learn complex behaviors. You will examine what is meant by nonlinear behaviors in Chapter 2. We will study some of the commonly used functions now.

1.4.7.1 Sigmoid function

The Sigmoid function is a bounded monotonic mathematical function. It is a differentiable function with an S-shaped curve, and its first derivative function is bell shaped. It has a nonnegative derivative function and is defined for all real input values. The Sigmoid function is used if the output value of a neuron is between 0 and 1.

Mathematically, a sigmoid function is as shown in Equation 1-1.

$$S(x) = \frac{1}{1+e^{-x}} = \frac{e^x}{e^x+1} \qquad \text{(Equation 1-1)}$$

The graph of a sigmoid function can be seen in Figure 1-11. Note the shape of the function and the max and min values.

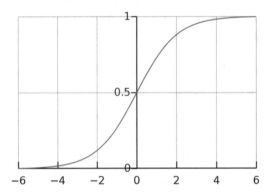

Figure 1-11. *A Sigmoid function; note it is not zero centered, and its values lie between 0 and 1. A sigmoid suffers from the problem of vanishing gradients*

A Sigmoid function finds its applications in complex learning systems. Often you would find a Sigmoid function is being used when a specific mathematical model is not fitting. It is usually used for binary classification and in the final output layer of the network. A Sigmoid function suffers from a vanishing gradient problem which we will discuss in subsequent sections.

1.4.7.2 tanh function

In mathematics, the tangent hyperbolic function or tanh is a differentiable hyperbolic function. It is a scaled version of the Sigmoid function. It is a smooth function, and its input values are in the range of –1 to +1.

With more stable gradients, it has fewer vanishing gradient problems than the Sigmoid function. A tanh function can be represented as Figure 1-12 and can be seen in Equation 1-2.

$$Tanh(x) = \frac{e^x - e^{-x}}{e^x + e^{-x}} \qquad \text{(Equation 1-2)}$$

A graphical representation of tanh is also shown. Note the difference between the Sigmoid and tanh function. Observe how tanh is a scaled version of the Sigmoid function.

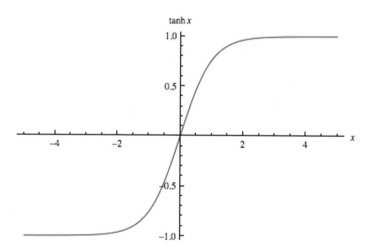

Figure 1-12. *A tanh function; note it passes through zero and is a scaled version of the sigmoid function. Its value lies between –1 and +1. Similar to sigmoid, tanh suffers from a vanishing gradient problem too*

A tanh function is generally used in the hidden layers. It makes the mean closer to zero which makes the training easier for the next layer in the network. This is also referred to as *centering the data*. A tanh function can be derived from the Sigmoid function and vice versa. Similar to sigmoid, the tanh function suffers from a vanishing gradient problem which we will discuss in subsequent sections.

We now examine the most popular activation function – ReLU.

1.4.7.3 Rectified Linear Unit or ReLU

The Rectified Linear Unit or ReLU is an activation function that defines the positives of an argument.

ReLU is a simple function, least expensive to compute, and can be trained much faster. It is unbounded and not centered at zero. It is differentiable at all the places except zero. Since a ReLU function can be trained much faster, you will find it to be used more frequently.

We can examine the ReLU function and the graph in Figure 1-13. The equation can be seen in Equation 1-3. Note that the value is 0 even for the negative values, and from 0 the value starts to incline.

$F(x) = \max(0, x)$ i.e. will give output as x if positive else 0   (Equation 1-3)

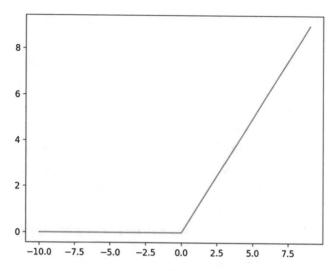

Figure 1-13. *A ReLU function; note it is quite simple to compute and hence faster in training. It is used in the hidden layers of the network. A ReLU is faster to train than sigmoid and tanh*

Since the ReLU function is less complex, is computationally less expensive, and hence is widely used in the hidden layers to train the networks faster, we will also use ReLU while designing the network. Now we study the softmax function which is used in the final layer of a network.

1.4.7.4 Softmax function

The softmax function is used in the final layer of the Neural Network to generate the output from the network. The output can be a final classification of an image for distinct categories.

The softmax function calculates the probabilities for each of the target classes over all the possibilities. It is an activation function that is useful for multiclass classification problems and forces the Neural Network to output the sum of 1.

As an example, if the input is [1,2,3,4,4,3,2,1] and we take a softmax, then the corresponding output will be [0.024, 0.064, 0.175, 0.475, 0.024, 0.064, 0.175]. This output is allocating the highest weight to the highest value which is 4 in this case. And hence it can be used to highlight the highest value. A more practical example will be if the number of distinct classes for an image are cars, bikes, or trucks, the softmax function will generate three probabilities for each category. The category which has received the highest probability will be the predicted category.

We have studied the important activation functions. But there can be other activation functions like Leaky ReLU, ELU, and so on. We will encounter these activation functions throughout the book. Table 1-1 shows a summary of the activation functions for quick reference.

Table 1-1. *The major activation functions and their respective details*

Activation Function	Value	Positives	Challenges
Sigmoid	[0,1]	(1) Nonlinear (2) Easy to work with (3) Continuous differentiable (4) Monotonic and does not blow up the activations	(1) Output not zero centered (2) Problem of vanishing gradients (3) Is slow to train
tanh	[-1,1]	(1) Similar to the sigmoid function (2) Gradient is stronger but is preferred over sigmoid	(1) Problem of vanishing gradient

(continued)

Table 1-1. (*continued*)

Activation Function	Value	Positives	Challenges
ReLU	[0,inf]	(1) Not linear (2) Easy to compute and hence fast to train (3) Resolves problem of vanishing gradient	(1) Used only in the hidden layers (2) Can blow up the activations (3) For the x<0 region, the gradient will be zero. Hence, weights do not get updated (dying ReLU problem)
Leaky ReLU	max(0,x)	(1) A variant of ReLU (2) Fixes dying ReLU problem	(1) Cannot be used for complex classifications
ELU	[0,inf]	(1) Alternative to ReLU (2) The output is smoother	(1) Can blow up the activations
Softmax	Calculates probabilities	Generally used in the output layer	

Activation functions form the core building block of a network. In the next section, we discuss the learning rate which guides how the network is going to learn and optimize the training.

1.4.8 Learning rate

For a Neural Network, the *learning rate* will define the size of the corrective steps which a model takes to reduce the errors. A higher learning rate has lower accuracy but a shorter time to train, while a lower learning rate will take a long time to train but have higher accuracy. You have to arrive at the most optimized value of it.

Specifically put, learning rate will govern the adjustments to be made to the weights during training of the network. Learning rate will directly impact the amount of time it will take for the network to converge and reach the global minima. In most of the cases, having a learning rate of 0.01 is acceptable.

We will now explore perhaps the most important process in the training process – the backpropagation algorithm.

1.4.9 Backpropagation

We studied about the learning rate in the last section. The objective of the training process is to reduce the error in the predictions. While the learning rate defines the size of the corrective steps to reduce the error, backpropagation is used to adjust the connection weights. These weights are updated backward based on the error. Following it, the errors are recalculated, gradient descent is calculated, and the respective weights are adjusted.

Figure 1-14 shows the process for backpropagation where the information flows from the output layer back to the hidden layers. Note that the flow of information is backwards as compared to forward propagation where the information flows from left to right.

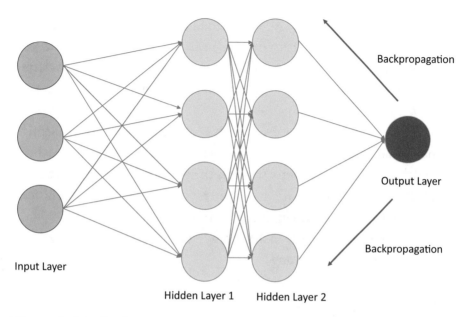

Figure 1-14. *Backpropagation in a Neural Network. Based on the error the information flows from the output backward, and subsequently weights are recalculated*

Let us explore the process in more detail.

Once the network makes a prediction, we can calculate the error which is the difference between the expected and the predicted value. This is referred to as the cost function. Based on the value of cost, the Neural Network then adjusts its weights and biases to get closest to the actual values or, in other words, minimize the error. This is done during backpropagation.

Note   You are advised to refresh differential calculus to understand the backpropagation algorithm better.

During backpropagation, the parameters of the connections are repeatedly and iteratively updated and adjusted. The level of adjustments is determined by the gradient of the cost function with respect to those parameters. The gradient will tell us in which direction should we adjust the weights to minimize the cost. And these gradients are calculated using the chain rule. Using the chain rule, the gradients are calculated for one layer at a time, iterating backward from the last layer to the first layer. This is done to avoid redundant calculations of intermediate terms in the chain rule.

Sometimes, we encounter the problem of vanishing gradients during the training of a Neural Network. The vanishing gradient problem is the phenomenon when the initial layers of the network cease to learn as the gradient becomes close to zero. It makes the network unstable, and the initial layers of the network will not be able to learn anything. We will again explore vanishing gradients in Chapters 6 and 8.

We now discuss the issue of overfitting – one of the most common problems faced during training.

1.4.10 Overfitting

You know that training data is used by a network to learn the attributes and patterns. But we want our Machine Learning models to perform well on unseen data so that we can use it to make the predictions.

To measure the accuracy of Machine Learning, we have to evaluate the performance of both training and testing datasets. Often, the network mimics the training data well and gets good training accuracy, whereas on the testing/validation dataset, the accuracy drops. This is called *overfitting*. Simply put, if the network is working well on the training dataset but not so great on unseen dataset, it is called overfitting.

Overfitting is a nuisance, and we have to fight it, right? To tackle overfitting, you can train your network with more training data. Or reduce the networks' complexity. By reducing the complexity, we suggest to reduce the number of weights, the value of weights, or the structure of the network itself.

Batch normalization and *Dropout* are two other techniques to mitigate the problem of overfitting.

Batch normalization is a type of regularization method. It is the process of normalizing the output from a layer with zero mean and a standard deviation of one. It reduces the emphasis on the weight initialization and hence reduces overfitting.

Dropout is another technique to fight the problem of overfitting. It is a regularization method. During training, the output of some layers is randomly dropped out or neglected. The effect is that we get different neural nets for each combination. It makes the training process noisy too. Figure 1-15 represents the impact of Dropout. The first figure on the left (Figure 1-15(i)) is a standard Neural Network. The one on the right (Figure 1-15(ii)) is the result after Dropout.

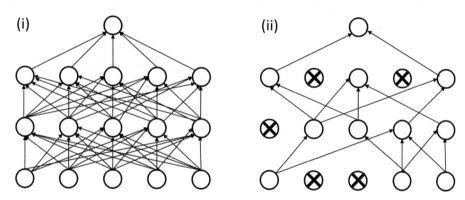

Figure 1-15. *Before dropout, the network might suffer from overfitting. After dropout, random connections and neurons are removed, and hence the network will not suffer from overfitting*

With dropout, we can tackle overfitting in our network and reach a much more robust solution.

Next, we will study the process of optimization using gradient descent.

1.4.11 Gradient descent

The purpose of a Machine Learning solution is to find the most optimum value for our. We want to decrease the loss during the training phase or maximize the accuracy. Gradient descent can help to achieve this purpose.

Gradient descent is used to find the global minimum or global maximum of a function. It is a highly used optimization technique. We proceed in the direction of the steepest descent iteratively which is defined by the negative of the gradient.

But gradient descent can be slow to run on very large datasets. It is due to the fact that one iteration of the gradient descent algorithm predicts for every instance in the training dataset. Hence, it is obvious that it will take a lot of time if we have thousands of records. For such a situation, we have *Stochastic Gradient Descent*.

In Stochastic Gradient Descent, rather than at the end of the batch, the coefficients are updated for each training instance, and hence it takes less time.

Figure 1-16 shows the way a gradient descent works. Notice how we can progress downward toward the global minimum.

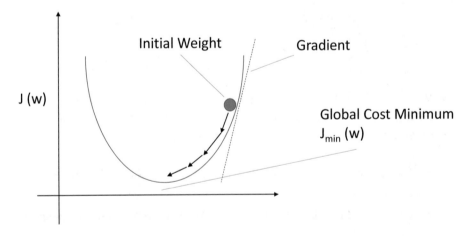

Figure 1-16. *The concept of gradient descent; notice how it aims to reach the global minimum. The objective of training the network is to minimize the error encountered*

We examined how we optimize the function using gradient descent. The way to check for the efficacy of the machine learning model is to measure how far or how close the predictions are to the actual values. And that is defined using loss which we discuss now.

1.4.12 Loss functions

Loss is the measure of our model's accuracy. In simple terms, it is the difference of actual and predicted values. The function which is used to calculate this loss is called the *loss function.*

Different loss functions give different values for the same loss. And since the loss is different, the respective model's performance will differ too.

We have different loss functions for regression and classification problems. Cross-entropy is used to define a loss function for the optimization. To measure the error between the actual output and the desired output, generally, the mean squared error is used. Some researchers suggest to use the cross-entropy error instead of the mean squared error. Table 1-2 gives a quick summary for different loss functions.

Table 1-2. *The various loss functions which can be used with their respective equations and the usage*

Loss Function	Equation for the Loss	Used for
Cross-entropy	-y(log(p) + (1-y) log(1-p))	Classification
Hinge loss	max(0, 1- y *f(x))	Classification
Absolute error	|y - f(x)|	Regression
Squared error	(y - f(x))^2	Regression
Huber loss	L_δ = ½ (y - f(x))^2 , if |y-f(x)| <= δ else δ|y-f(x)| - ½ δ^2	Regression

We have now examined the main concepts of Deep Learning. Now let us study how a Neural Network works. We will understand how the various layers interact with each other and how information is passed from one layer to another.

Let's get started!

1.5 How Deep Learning works?

You now know that a Deep Learning network has various layers. And you have also gone through the concepts of Deep Learning. You may be wondering how these pieces come together and orchestrate the entire learning. The entire process can be examined as follows:

Step 1

You may be wondering what a layer actually does, what a layer achieves, and what is stored in the respective weights of a layer. It is nothing but a set of numbers. Technically, it is imperative that the transformation implemented by a layer is parameterized by its weights which are also referred to as parameters of a layer.

And what is meant by learning is the next question. Learning for a Neural Network is finding the best combination and values for weights for all the layers of the network so that we can achieve the best accuracy. As deep Neural Networks can have many values of such parameters, we have to find the most optimum value for all the parameters. This seems like a herculean task considering that changing one value impacts others.

Let us show the process in the Neural Network by means of a diagram (Figure 1-17). Examine our input data layer. Two data transformation layers each having respective weights associated with them. And then we have a final prediction for the target variable Y.

The images are fed into the input layer and then are transformed in the data transformation layers.

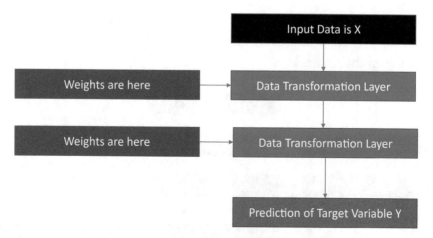

Figure 1-17. *The input data is transformed in the data transformation layers, weights are defined, and the initial prediction is made*

Step 2

We have created a basic skeleton in step 1. Now we have to gauge the accuracy of this network.

We would want to control the output of a Neural Network; we have to compare and contrast the accuracy of the output.

Info   Accuracy will refer to how far our prediction is from the actual value. Simply put, how good or bad our predictions are from the real values is a measure of accuracy.

Accuracy measurement is done by the loss function of the network, also called the *objective function*. The loss function takes the predictions of the network and the true or actual target values. These actual values are what we expected the network to output. The loss function computes a distance score, capturing how well the network has done.

Let's update the diagram we created in step 1 by adding a loss function and corresponding loss score (Figure 1-18). It helps to measure the accuracy for the network.

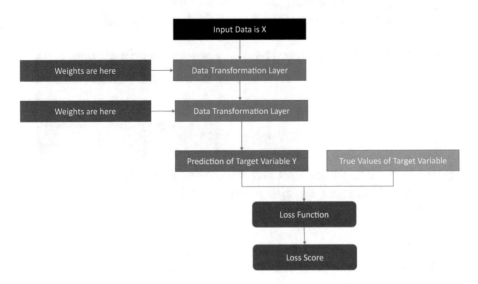

Figure 1-18. *Add a loss function to measure the accuracy; loss is the difference between actual and predicted values. At this stage, we know the performance of the network based on the error term*

Step 3

As we discussed earlier, we have to maximize the accuracy or lower the loss. This will make the solution robust and accurate in predictions.

In order to constantly lower the loss, the score (predictions – actual) is then used as a feedback signal to adjust the value of the weights a little which is done by the optimizer. This task is done by the *backpropagation algorithm* which is sometimes called the central algorithm in Deep Learning.

Initially, some random values are assigned to the weights, so the network is implementing a series of random transformations. And logically enough, the output is quite different from what we would be expecting, and the loss score is accordingly very high. After all, it is the very first attempt!

But this is going to improve. While training the Neural Network, we constantly encounter new training examples. And with each fresh example, the weights are adjusted a little in the correct direction, and subsequently the loss score decreases. We iterate this training loop many times, and it results in most optimum weight values that minimize the loss function.

We then achieve our objective which is a trained network with minimal loss. It means that actual and predicted values are very close to each other. To achieve the complete solution, we scale up this mechanism which is visible in Figure 1-19.

Notice the optimizer which provides regular and continuous feedback to reach the best solution.

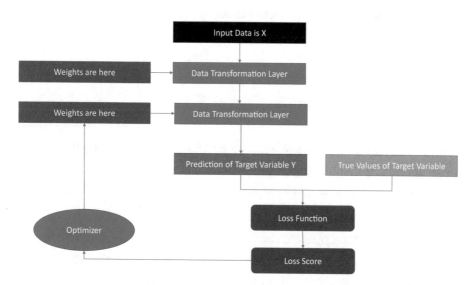

Figure 1-19. *Optimizer to give the feedback and optimize the weights; this is the process of backpropagation. It ensures that the error is reduced iteratively*

Once we have achieved the best values for our network, we call that our network is trained now. We can now use it to make predictions on unseen datasets.

Now you have understood what the various components of Deep Learning are and how they work together. It is time for you to now examine all the tools and libraries for Deep Learning.

1.5.1 Popular Deep Learning libraries

There are quite a few Deep Learning libraries which are available. These packages allow us to develop solutions faster and with minimum efforts as most of the heavy lifting is done by these libraries.

We are discussing the most popular libraries here.

TensorFlow: TensorFlow (TF) developed by Google is arguably one of the most popular and widely used Deep Learning frameworks. It was launched in 2015 and since is being used by a number of businesses and brands across the globe.

Python is mostly used for TF, but C++, Java, C#, JavaScript, and Julia can also be used. You have to install the TF library on your system and import the library. And it is ready to be used!

Note   Go to www.tensorflow.org/install and follow the instructions to install TensorFlow.

A TF model has to be retrained in case of any modifications to the model architecture. It operates with a static computation graph which means we define the graph first, and then the calculations are run.

It is quite popular as it's developed by Google. It can work on mobile devices like iOS and Android too.

Keras: It is one of the easiest Deep Learning frameworks for starters and fantastic for understanding and prototyping simple concepts. Keras was initially released in 2015 and is one of the most recommended libraries to understand the nuances of Neural Networks.

Note   Go to `https://keras.io` and follow the instructions to install Keras. Tf.keras can be used as an API and will be used frequently in this book.

It is a mature API-driven solution. Prototyping in Keras is facilitated to the limit. Serialization/deserialization APIs, callbacks, and data streaming using Python generators are very mature. Massive models in Keras are reduced to single-line functions which makes it a less configurable environment.

PyTorch: Facebook's brain-child PyTorch was released in 2016 and is one of the popular Deep Learning libraries. We can use debuggers in PyTorch, for example, pdb or PyCharm. PyTorch operates with dynamically updated graphs and allows data parallelism and distributed learning models. For small projects and prototyping, PyTorch should be your choice; however, for cross-platform solutions, TensorFlow is known to be better.

Sonnet: DeepMind's Sonnet is developed using and on top of TF. Sonnet is designed for complex Neural Network applications and architectures.

Sonnet creates primary Python objects which correspond to a particular part of the Neural Network (NN). After this, these Python objects are connected independently to the computational TensorFlow graph. It simplifies the design which is due to the separation of the process of creating objects and associating them with a graph. Further, the capability to have high-level object-oriented libraries is advantageous as it helps in abstraction when we develop Machine Learning algorithms.

MXNet: Apache's MXNet is a highly scalable Deep Learning tool that is easy to use and has detailed documentation. A large number of languages like C++, Python, R, Julia, JavaScript, Scala, Go, and Perl are supported by MXNet.

There are other frameworks too like Swift, Gluon, Chainer, DL4J, and so on; however, we've only discussed the popular ones in this book. Table 1-3 gives an overview of all the frameworks.

Table 1-3. *Major Deep Learning frameworks and their respective attributes*

Framework	Source	Attributes
TensorFlow	Open source	Most popular, can work on mobile too, TensorBoard provides visualizations
Keras	Open source	API-driven mature solution, very easy to use
PyTorch	Open source	Allows data parallelism and very good for quick product building
Sonnet	Open source	Simplified design, creates high-level object
MXNet	Open source	Highly scalable, easy to use
MATLAB	Licensed	Highly configurable, provides deployment capabilities

1.6 Summary

Deep Learning is a continuous learning experience and requires discipline, rigor, and commitment. You have taken the first step in your learning journey. In this first chapter, we studied concepts of Image Processing and Deep Learning. They are the building blocks for the entire book and your path ahead. We developed three solutions using OpenCV.

In the next chapter, you will deep dive into TensorFlow and Keras. And you will develop your first solution using Convolutional Neural Network. Right from designing the network, training it, and implementing it. So stay focused!

REVIEW EXERCISES

1. What are the various steps in Image Processing?

2. Develop an object detection solution using OpenCV.

3. What is the process of training a Deep Learning network?

4. What is overfitting and how do we tackle it?

5. What are various activation functions?

1.6.1 Further readings

1. A brief introduction to OpenCV: `https://ieeexplore.ieee.org/document/6240859`.

2. OpenCV for computer vision applications: `www.researchgate.net/publication/301590571_OpenCV_for_Computer_Vision_Applications`.

3. OpenCV documentation can be accessed at `https://docs.opencv.org/`.

4. Go through these following papers:

   a. `www.usenix.org/system/files/conference/osdi16/osdi16-abadi.pdf`

   b. `https://arxiv.org/pdf/1404.7828.pdf`

CHAPTER 2

Nuts and Bolts of Deep Learning for Computer Vision

The mind is not a vessel to be filled, but a fire to be kindled.

—Plutarch

We humans are blessed with extraordinary powers of mind. These powers allow us to differentiate and distinguish, develop new skills, learn new arts, and make rational decisions. Our visual powers have no limits. We can recognize faces regardless of pose and background. We can distinguish objects like cars, dogs, tables, phones, and so on irrespective of the brand and type. We can recognize colors and shapes and distinguish clearly and easily between them. This power is developed periodically and systematically. In our young age, we continuously learn the attributes of objects and develop our knowledge. That information is kept safe in our memory. With time, this knowledge and learning improve. This is such an astonishing process that iteratively trains our eyes and minds. It is often argued that Deep Learning originated as a mechanism to mimic these extraordinary powers. In computer vision, Deep Learning is helping us to uncover the capabilities which can be used to help organizations use

© Vaibhav Verdhan 2021
V. Verdhan, *Computer Vision Using Deep Learning,*
https://doi.org/10.1007/978-1-4842-6616-8_2

computer vision for productive purposes. Deep Learning has evolved a lot and is still having a lot of scope for further progress.

In the first chapter, we started with fundamentals of Deep Learning. In this second chapter, we will build on those fundamentals, go deeper, understand the various layers of a Neural Network, and create a Deep Learning solution using Keras and Python.

We will cover the following topics in this chapter:

(1)   What is tensor and how to use TensorFlow

(2)   Demystifying Convolutional Neural Network

(3)   Components of convolutional Neural Network

(4)   Developing CNN network for image classification

2.1 Technical requirements

The code and datasets for the chapter are uploaded at the GitHub link `https://github.com/Apress/computer-vision-using-deep-learning/ tree/main/Chapter2` for this book. We will use the Jupyter Notebook. For this chapter, a CPU is good enough to execute the code, but if required you can use Google Colaboratory. You can refer to the reference at the end of the book, if you are not able to set up the Google Colab yourself.

2.2 Deep Learning using TensorFlow and Keras

Let us examine TensorFlow (TF) and Keras briefly now. They are arguably the most common open source libraries.

TensorFlow (TF) is a platform for Machine Learning by Google. *Keras* is a framework developed on top of other DL toolkits like TF, Theano, CNTK, and so on. It has built-in support for convolutional and recurrent Neural Networks.

Tip   Keras is an API-driven solution; most of the heavy lifting is already done in Keras. It is easier to use and hence recommended for beginners.

The computations in TF are done using data flow graphs wherein the data is represented by edges (which are nothing but tensors or multidimensional data arrays) and nodes that represent mathematical operations. So, what exactly are tensors?

2.3 What is a tensor?

Recall *scalars* and *vectors* from your high-school mathematics. Vectors can be visualized as scalars with a direction. For example, a speed of 50 km/hr is a scalar, while 50 km/hr in the north direction is a vector. This means that a vector is a scalar magnitude in a given direction. A *tensor*, on the other hand, will be in multiple directions, that is, scalar magnitudes in multiple directions.

In terms of a mathematical definition, a tensor is an object that can provide a linear mapping between two algebraic objects. These objects can themselves be scalars or vectors or even tensors.

A tensor can be visualized in a vector space diagram as shown in Figure 2-1.

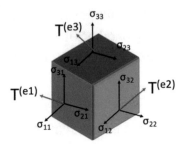

Figure 2-1. *A tensor represented in a vector space diagram. A tensor is a scalar magnitude in multiple directions and is used to provide linear mapping between two algebraic objects*

As you can see in Figure 2-1, a tensor has projections across multiple directions. A tensor can be thought of as a mathematical entity, which is described using components. They are described with reference to a basis, and if this associated basis changes, the tensor has to change itself. An example is coordinate change; if a transformation is done on the basis, the tensor's numeric value will also change. TensorFlow uses these tensors to make complex computations.

Now let's develop a basic check to see if you have installed TF correctly. We are going to multiply two constants to check if the installation is correct.

Info   Refer to Chapter 1 if you want to know how to install TensorFlow and Keras.

---

1. Let's import TensorFlow:

    ```
    import tensorflow as tf
    ```

2. Initialize two constants:

    ```
    a = tf.constant([1,1,1,1])
    b = tf.constant([2,2,2,2])
    ```

3. Multiply the two constants:

```
product_results = tf.multiply(a, b)
```

4. Print the final result:

```
print(product_results)
```

If you are able to get the results, congratulations you are all set to go!

Now let us study a Convolutional Neural Network in detail. After that, you will be ready to create your first image classification model.

Exciting, right?

2.3.1 What is a Convolutional Neural Network?

When we humans see an image or a face, we are able to identify it immediately. It is one of the basic skills we have. This identification process is an amalgamation of a large number of small processes and coordination between various vital components of our visual system.

A Convolutional Neural Network or CNN is able to replicate this astounding capability using Deep Learning.

Consider this. We have to create a solution to distinguish between a cat and a dog. The attributes which make them different can be ears, whiskers, nose, and so on. CNNs are helpful for extracting the attributes of the images which are significant for the images. Or in other words, CNNs will extract the features which are distinguishing between a cat and a dog. CNNs are very powerful in image classification, object detection, object tracking, image captioning, face recognition, and so on.

Let us dive into the concepts of CNN. We will examine convolution first.

2.3.2 What is convolution?

The primary objective of the convolution process is to extract features which are important for image classification, object detection, and so on. The features will be edges, curves, color drops, lines and so on. Once the process has been trained well, it will learn these attributes at a significant point in the image. And then it can detect it later in any part of the image.

Imagine you have an image of size 32x32. That means it can be represented as 32x32x3 pixels if it is a colored image (remember RGB). Now let us move (or *convolute*) an area of 5x5 over this image and cover the entire image. This process is called *convolving*. Starting from the top left, this area is passed over the entire image. You can refer to Figure 2-2 to see how an image 32x32 is being convoluted by a filter of 5x5.

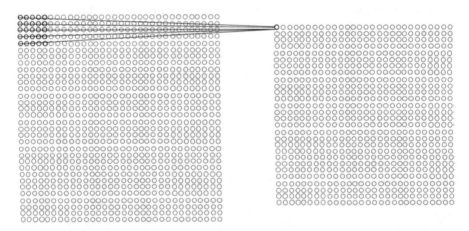

Figure 2-2. *Convolution process: input layer is on the left, output is on the right. The 32x32 image is being convoluted by a filter of size 5x5*

The 5x5 area which is passed over the entire image is called a *filter* which is sometimes called a *kernel* or *feature detector*. The region which is highlighted in Figure 2-2 is called the filter's *receptive field*. Hence, we can say that a filter is just a matrix with values called weights. These weights are trained and updated during the model training process. This filter moves over each and every part of the image.

We can understand the convolutional process by means of an example of the complete process as shown in Figure 2-3. The original image is 5x5 in size, and the filter is 3x3 in size. The filter moves over the entire image and keeps on generating the output.

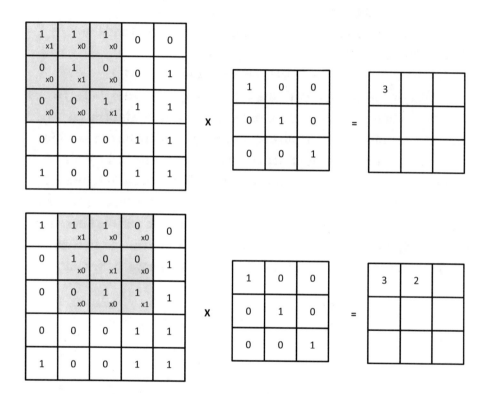

Figure 2-3. *Convolution is the process where the element-wise product and the addition are done. In the first image, the output is 3, and in the second image, the filter has shifted one place to the right and the output is 2*

In Figure 2-3, the 3x3 filter is convolving over the entire image. The filter checks if the feature it meant to detect is present or not. The filter carries a convolution process, which is the element-wise product and sum between the two metrics. If a feature is present, the convolution output of the filter and the part of the image will result in a high number. If the feature is not present, the output will be low. Hence, this output value represents how confident a filter is that a particular feature is present in the image.

We move this filter over the entire image, resulting in an output matrix called feature maps or activation maps. This feature map will have the convolutions of the filter over the entire image.

Let's say the dimensions of the input image are (n,n) and the dimensions of filter are (x,x).

So, the output after the CNN layer is **((n-x+1), (n-x+1))**.

Hence, in the example in Figure 2-3, the output is (5-3+1, 5-3+1) = (3,3).

There is one more component called *channels* which is of much interest. Channels are the depth of matrices involved in the convolution process. The filter will be applied to each of the channels in the input image. We are again representing the output of the process in Figure 2-4. The input image is 5x5x5 in size, and we have a filter of 3x3x3. The output hence becomes an image of size (3x3). We should note that the filter should have exactly the same number of channels as the input image. In Figure 2-4, it is 3. It is to allow the element-wise multiplication between the metrics.

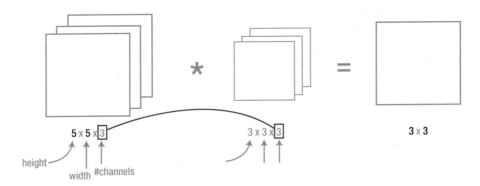

Figure 2-4. *The filter has the same number of channels as the input image*

There is one more component which we should be aware of. The filter can slide over the input image at varying intervals. It is referred to as the *stride value*, and it suggests how much the filter should move at each of the steps.

The process is shown in Figure 2-5. In the first figure on the left, we have a single stride, while on the right, a two-stride movement has been shown.

1	0	1	0	1
0	1	0	1	0
1	0	0	1	1
0	1	0	0	1
1	0	0	0	1

1	0	1	0	1
0	1	0	1	0
1	0	0	1	1
0	1	0	0	1
1	0	0	0	1

1	0	1	0	1
0	1	0	1	0
1	0	0	1	1
0	1	0	0	1
1	0	0	0	1

1	0	1	0	1
0	1	0	1	0
1	0	0	1	1
0	1	0	0	1
1	0	0	0	1

Figure 2-5. *Stride suggests how much the filter should move at each step. The figure shows the impact of a stride on convolution. In the first figure, we have a stride of 1, while in the second image, we have a stride of 2*

You would agree that with the convolution process, we will quickly lose the pixels along the periphery. As we have seen in Figure 2-3, a 5x5 image became a 3x3 image, and this loss will increase with a greater number of layers. To tackle this problem, we have the concept of padding. In padding, we add some pixels to an image which is getting processed. For example, we can pad the image with zeros as shown in Figure 2-6. The usage of padding results in a better analysis and better results from the convolutional Neural Networks.

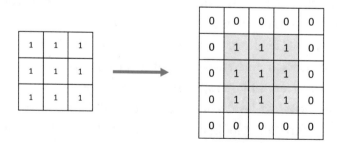

Figure 2-6. *Zero padding has been added to the input image. Convolution as the process reduces the number of pixels, padding allows us to tackle it*

Now we have understood the prime components of a CNN. Let us combine the concepts and create a small process. If we have an image of size (nxn) and we apply a filter of size "f," with a stride of "s" and padding "s," then the output of the process will be

$$((n+2p - f)/s +1), (n+2p - f)/s +1))$$ (Equation 2-1)

We can understand the process as shown in Figure 2-7. We have an input image of size 37x37 and a filter of size 3x3, and the number of filters is 10, the stride is 1, and the padding is 0. Based on Equation 2-1, the output will be 35x35x10.

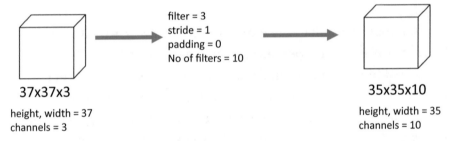

Figure = 3
stride = 1
padding = 0
No of filters = 10

37x37x3

height, width = 37
channels = 3

35x35x10

height, width = 35
channels = 10

Figure 2-7. *A convolution process in which we have a filter of size 3x3, stride of 1, padding of 0, and number of filters as 10*

Convolution helps us in extracting the significant attributes of the image. The layers of the network closer to the origin (the input image) learn the low-level features, while the final layers learn the higher features. In the initial layers of the network, features like edges, curves, and so on are getting extracted, while the deeper layers will learn about the resulting shapes from these low-level features like face, object, and so on.

But this computation looks complex, isn't it? And as the network will go deep, this complexity will increase. So how do we deal with it? Pooling layer is the answer. Let's understand it.

2.3.3 What is a Pooling Layer?

The CNN layer which we studied results in a feature map of the input. But as the network becomes deeper, this computation becomes complex. It is due to the reason that with each layer and neuron, the number of dimensions in the network increases. And hence the overall complexity of the network increases.

And, there's one more challenge: any image augmentation will change the feature map. For example, a rotation will change the position of a feature in the image, and hence the respective feature map will also change.

Note   Often, you will face nonavailability of raw data. Image augmentation is one of the recommended methods to create new images for you which can serve as training data.

This change in the feature map can be addressed by *downsampling*. In downsampling, a lower resolution of the input image is created, and the *Pooling Layer* helps us with this.

A Pooling Layer is added after the Convolutional Layer. Each of the feature maps is operated upon individually, and we get a new set of pooled feature maps. The size of this operation filter is smaller than the feature map's size.

A pooling layer is generally applied after the convolutional layer. A pooling layer with 3x3 pixels and a stride diminishes feature maps' size by a factor of 2 which means that each dimension is halved. For example, if we apply a pooling layer to a feature map of 8x8 (64 pixels), the output will be a feature map of 4x4 (16 pixels).

There are two types of Pooling Layers.

Average Pooling and Max Pooling. The former calculates the average of each value of the feature map, while the latter gets the maximum value for each patch of the feature map. Let us examine them as shown in Figure 2-8.

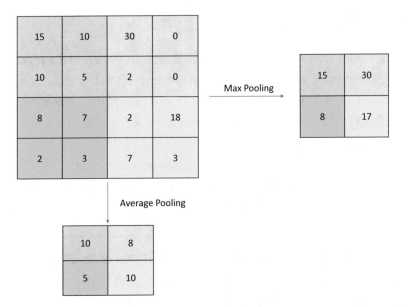

Figure 2-8. *The right figure is the max pooling, while the bottom is the average pooling*

As you can see in Figure 2-8, the average pooling layer does an average of the four numbers, while the max pooling selects the maximum from the four numbers.

There is one more important concept about Fully Connected layers which you should know before you are equipped to create a CNN model. Let us examine it and then you are good to go.

2.3.4 What is a Fully Connected Layer?

A Fully Connected layer takes input from the outputs of the preceding layer (activation maps of high-level features) and outputs an n-dimensional vector. Here, n is the number of distinct classes.

For example, if the objective is to ascertain if an image is of a horse, a fully connected layer will have high-level features like tail, legs, and so on in the activation maps. A fully connected layer looks like Figure 2-9.

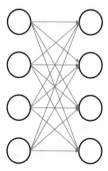

Figure 2-9. *A fully connected layer is depicted here*

A Fully Connected layer will look at the features which correspond most closely to a particular class and have particular weights. This is done to get correct probabilities for different classes when we get the product between the weights and the previous layer.

Now you have understood CNN and its components. It is time to hit the code. You will create your first Deep Learning solution to classify between cats and dogs. All the very best!

2.4 Developing a DL solution using CNN

We will now create a Deep Learning solution using CNN. The "Hello World" of Deep Learning is generally called an MNIST dataset. It is a collection of handwritten numerical digits as depicted in Figure 2-10.

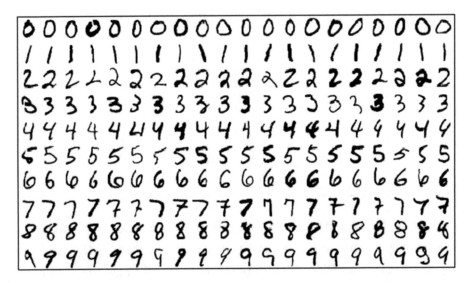

Figure 2-10. *MNIST dataset: "Hello World" for image recognition*

There is a famous paper on recognizing MNIST images (description is given at the end of the chapter). To avoid repetition, we are uploading the entire code at GitHub. You are advised to check the code.

We will now start creating the image classification model!

In this first Deep Learning solution, we want to distinguish between a cat and a dog based on their image. The dataset is available at www.kaggle. com/c/dogs-vs-cats.

The steps to be followed are listed here:

1. First, let's build the dataset:

    a. Download the dataset from Kaggle. Unzip the dataset.

    b. You will find two folders: test and train. Delete the test folder as we will create our own test folder.

    c. Inside both the train and test folders, create two subfolders – cats and dogs – and put the images in the respective folders.

    d.   Take some images (I took 2000) from the "train>cats" folder and put them in the "test>cats" folder.

    e.   Take some images (I took 2000) from the "train>dogs" folder and put them in the "test>dogs" folder.

    f.   Your dataset is ready to be used.

2.   Import the required libraries now. We will import `sequential`, `pooling`, `activation`, and `flatten` layers from `keras`. Import `numpy` too.

Note   In the Reference of the book, we provide the description of each of the layers and their respective functions.

```
from keras.models import Sequential
from keras.layers import Conv2D,Activation,
MaxPooling2D,Dense,Flatten,Dropout
import numpy as np
```

3.   Initialize a model, `catDogImageclassifier` variable here:

```
catDogImageclassifier = Sequential()
```

4.   Now, we'll add layers to our network. Conv2D will add a two-dimensional convolutional layer which will have 32 filters. 3,3 represents the size of the filter (3 rows, 3 columns). The following input image shape is 64*64*3 – height*width*RGB. Each number represents the pixel intensity (0–255).

```
catDogImageclassifier.add(Conv2D(32,(3,3),
input_shape=(64,64,3)))
```

5. The output of the last layer will be a feature map. The training data will work on it and get some feature maps.

6. Let's add the activation function. We are using ReLU (Rectified Linear Unit) for this example. In the feature map output from the previous layer, the activation function will replace all the negative pixels with zero.

Note   Recall from the definition of ReLU; it is max(0,x). ReLU allows positive values while replaces negative values with 0. Generally, ReLU is used only in hidden layers.

```
catDogImageclassifier.add(Activation('relu'))
```

7. Now we add the Max Pooling layer as we do not want our network to be overly complex computationally.

```
catDogImageclassifier.add(MaxPooling2D
(pool_size =(2,2)))
```

8. Next, we add all three convolutional blocks. Each block has a Cov2D, ReLU, and Max Pooling Layer.

```
catDogImageclassifier.add(Conv2D(32,(3,3)))
catDogImageclassifier.add(Activation('relu'))
catDogImageclassifier.add(MaxPooling2D(pool_size =(2,2)))
catDogImageclassifier.add(Conv2D(32,(3,3)))
catDogImageclassifier.add(Activation('relu'))
catDogImageclassifier.add(MaxPooling2D(pool_size =(2,2)))
```

```
catDogImageclassifier.add(Conv2D(32,(3,3
catDogImageclassifier.add(Activation('relu'))
catDogImageclassifier.add(MaxPooling2D(pool_size
=(2,2)))
```

9. Now, let's flatten the dataset which will transform
   the pooled feature map matrix into one column.

```
catDogImageclassifier.add(Flatten())
```

10. Add the dense function now followed by the ReLU
    activation:

```
catDogImageclassifier.add(Dense(64))
catDogImageclassifier.add(Activation('relu'))
```

Info   Do you think why we need nonlinear functions like tanh, ReLU,
and so on? If you use only linear functions, the output will be linear
too. Hence, we use nonlinear functions in hidden layers.

---

11. Overfitting is a nuisance. We will add the Dropout
    layer to overcome overfitting next:

```
catDogImageclassifier.add(Dropout(0.5))
```

12. Add one more fully connected layer to get the output
    in n-dimensional classes (a vector will be the output).

```
catDogImageclassifier.add(Dense(1))
```

13. Add the Sigmoid function to convert to probabilities:

```
catDogImageclassifier.add(Activation('sigmoid'))
```

14. Let's print a summary of the network.

```
catDogImageclassifier.summary()
```

We see the entire network in the following image:

```
1  catDogImageclassifier.summary()
```

Layer (type)	Output Shape	Param #
conv2d_27 (Conv2D)	(None, 62, 62, 32)	896
activation_22 (Activation)	(None, 62, 62, 32)	0
max_pooling2d_20 (MaxPooling	(None, 31, 31, 32)	0
conv2d_28 (Conv2D)	(None, 29, 29, 32)	9248
activation_23 (Activation)	(None, 29, 29, 32)	0
max_pooling2d_21 (MaxPooling	(None, 14, 14, 32)	0
conv2d_29 (Conv2D)	(None, 12, 12, 32)	9248
activation_24 (Activation)	(None, 12, 12, 32)	0
max_pooling2d_22 (MaxPooling	(None, 6, 6, 32)	0
conv2d_30 (Conv2D)	(None, 4, 4, 32)	9248
activation_25 (Activation)	(None, 4, 4, 32)	0
max_pooling2d_23 (MaxPooling	(None, 2, 2, 32)	0
flatten_2 (Flatten)	(None, 128)	0
dense_3 (Dense)	(None, 64)	8256
activation_26 (Activation)	(None, 64)	0
dropout_2 (Dropout)	(None, 64)	0
dense_4 (Dense)	(None, 1)	65
activation_27 (Activation)	(None, 1)	0

```
Total params: 36,961
Trainable params: 36,961
Non-trainable params: 0
```

We can see the number of parameters in our network is 36,961. You are advised to play around with different network structures and gauge the impact.

15. Let us now compile the network. We use the optimizer rmsprop using gradient descent, and then we add the loss or the cost function.

```
catDogImageclassifier.compile(optimizer =
'rmsprop', loss ='binary_crossentropy',
metrics =['accuracy'])
```

16. Now we are doing data augmentation here (zoom, scale, etc.). It will also help to tackle the problem of overfitting. We use the ImageDataGenerator function to do this:

```
from keras.preprocessing.image import
ImageDataGenerator
train_datagen = ImageDataGenerator(rescale
=1./255, shear_range =0.25,zoom_range = 0.25,
horizontal_flip =True)
test_datagen = ImageDataGenerator(rescale =
1./255)
```

17. Load the training data:

```
training_set = train_datagen.flow_from_directory
('/Users/DogsCats/train',target_size=(64,6 4),
batch_size= 32,class_mode='binary')
```

18. Load the testing data:

```
test_set = test_datagen.flow_from_directory
('/Users/DogsCats/test', target_size = (64,64),
batch_size = 32,
class_mode ='binary')
```

19. Let us begin the training now.

```
from IPython.display import display
from PIL import Image catDogImageclassifier.fit_
generator(training_set, steps_per_epoch =625,
epochs = 10, validation_data =test_set,
validation_steps = 1000)
```

Steps per epoch are 625, and the number of epochs is 10. If we have 1000 images and a batch size of 10, the number of steps required will be 100 (1000/10).

Info   The number of *epochs* means the number of complete passes through the full training dataset. *Batch* is the number of training examples in a batch, while *iteration* is the number of batches needed to complete an epoch.

Depending on the complexity of the network, the number of epochs given, and so on, the compilation will take time. The test dataset is passed as a validation_data here.

The output is shown in Figure 2-11.

```
1  from IPython.display import display
2  from PIL import Image
3  catDogImageclassifier.fit_generator(training_set,
4                    steps_per_epoch =625,
5                    epochs = 10,
6                    validation_data =test_set,
7                    validation_steps = 1000)
```

```
Epoch 1/10
625/625 [==============================] - 185s 296ms/step - loss: 0.6721 - acc: 0.5822 - val_loss: 0.6069 - val_acc:
0.6610
Epoch 2/10
625/625 [==============================] - 152s 243ms/step - loss: 0.5960 - acc: 0.6831 - val_loss: 0.5151 - val_acc:
0.7543
Epoch 3/10
625/625 [==============================] - 151s 242ms/step - loss: 0.5452 - acc: 0.7217 - val_loss: 0.4891 - val_acc:
0.7545
Epoch 4/10
625/625 [==============================] - 150s 239ms/step - loss: 0.5069 - acc: 0.7568 - val_loss: 0.4657 - val_acc:
0.7743
Epoch 5/10
625/625 [==============================] - 150s 240ms/step - loss: 0.4813 - acc: 0.7713 - val_loss: 0.4407 - val_acc:
0.7925
Epoch 6/10
625/625 [==============================] - 152s 243ms/step - loss: 0.4526 - acc: 0.7866 - val_loss: 0.4374 - val_acc:
0.7924
Epoch 7/10
625/625 [==============================] - 151s 241ms/step - loss: 0.4458 - acc: 0.7953 - val_loss: 0.3891 - val_acc:
0.8324
Epoch 8/10
625/625 [==============================] - 151s 242ms/step - loss: 0.4177 - acc: 0.8123 - val_loss: 0.3917 - val_acc:
0.8221
Epoch 9/10
625/625 [==============================] - 155s 248ms/step - loss: 0.4158 - acc: 0.8158 - val_loss: 0.3947 - val_acc:
0.8176
Epoch 10/10
625/625 [==============================] - 151s 241ms/step - loss: 0.4021 - acc: 0.8201 - val_loss: 0.3783 - val_acc:
0.8221

<keras.callbacks.History at 0x1a376b5160>
```

Figure 2-11.   *Output of the training results for 10 epochs*

As seen in the results, in the final epoch, we got validation accuracy of 82.21%. We can also see that in Epoch 7 we got an accuracy of 83.24% which is better than the final accuracy.

We would then want to use the model created in Epoch 7 as the accuracy is best for it. We can achieve it by providing checkpoints between the training and saving that version. We will look at the process of creating and saving checkpoints in subsequent chapters.

We have saved the final model as a file here. The model can then be loaded again as and when required. The model will be saved as an HDF5 file, and it can be reused later.

```
catDogImageclassifier.save('catdog_cnn_model.h5')
```

20. Load the saved model using load_model:

```
from keras.models import load_model
catDogImageclassifier = load_model('catdog_
cnn_model.h5')
```

21. Check how the model is predicting an unseen
    image.

Here's the image (Figure 2-12) we are using to make a prediction. Feel
free to test the solution with different images.

Figure 2-12. *A dog image to test the accuracy of the model*

In the following code block, we make a prediction on the preceding
image using the model we have trained.

22. Load the library and the image from the folder. You
    would have to change the location of the file in code
    snippet below.

```
import numpy as np
from keras.preprocessing import image
an_image =image.load_img('/Users/vaibhavverdhan/Book
Writing/2.jpg',target_size =(64,64))
```

```
an_image =image.img_to_array(an_image)
```

Let us now expand the image's dimensions. It will improve the prediction power of the model. It is used to expand the shape of an array and inserts a new axis which appears at the position of the axis in the expanded array shape.

```
an_image =np.expand_dims(an_image, axis =0)
```

It is time to call the predict method now. We are setting the probability threshold at 0.5. You are advised to test on multiple thresholds and check the corresponding accuracy.

```
verdict = catDogImageclassifier.predict(an_image) if verdict[0]
[0] >= 0.5:
prediction = 'dog'
else:
prediction = 'cat'
```

23. Let us print our final prediction.

```
print(prediction)
```

The model predicts that the image is of a "dog."

Here, in this example, we designed a Neural Network using Keras. We trained the images using images of cats and dogs and tested it. It is possible to train a multiclassifier system too if we can get the images for each of the classes.

Congratulations! You just now finished your second image classification use case using Deep Learning. Use it for training your own image datasets. It is even possible to create a multiclass classification model.

Now you may think how you will use this model to make predictions in real time. The compiled model file (e.g., `'catdog_cnn_model.h5'`) will be deployed onto a server to make the predictions. We will be covering model deployment in detail in the last chapter of this book.

With this, we come to the close of the second chapter. You can proceed to the summary now.

2.5 Summary

Images are a rich source of information and knowledge. We can solve a lot of business problems by analyzing the image dataset. CNNs are leading the AI revolution particularly for images and videos. They are being used in the medical industry, manufacturing, retail, BFSI, and so on. Quite a few researches are going on using CNN.

CNN-based solutions are quite innovative and unique. There are a lot of challenges which have to be tackled while designing an innovative CNN-based solution. The choice of the number of layers, number of neurons in each layer, activation functions to be used, loss function, optimizer, and so on is not a straightforward one. It depends on the complexity of the business problem, the dataset at hand, and the available computation power. The efficacy of the solution depends a lot on the dataset available. If we have a clearly defined business objective which is measurable, precise, and achievable, if we have a representative and complete dataset, and if we have enough computation power, a lot of business problems can be addressed using Deep Learning.

In the first chapter of the book, we introduced computer vision and Deep Learning. In this second chapter, we studied concepts of convolutional, pooling, and fully connected layers. You are going to use these concepts throughout your journey. And you also developed an image classification model using Deep Learning.

The difficulty level is going to increase from the next chapter onward when we start with network architectures. Network architectures use the building blocks we have studied in the first two chapters. They are developed by scientists and researchers across organizations and universities to solve complex problems. We are going to study those networks and develop Python solutions too. So stay hungry!

You should be able to answer the questions in the exercise now!

REVIEW QUESTIONS

You are advised to solve these questions:

1. What is the convolution process in CNN and how is the output calculated?

2. Why do we need nonlinear functions in hidden layers?

3. What is the difference between max and average pooling?

4. What do you mean by dropout?

5. Download the image data of natural scenes around the world from www.kaggle.com/puneet6060/intel-image-classification and develop an image classification model using CNN.

6. Download the Fashion MNIST dataset from https://github.com/zalandoresearch/fashion-mnist and develop an image classification model.

2.5.1 Further readings

You are advised to go through the following papers:

1. Go through "Assessing Four Neural Networks on Handwritten Digit Recognition Dataset (MNIST)" at https://arxiv.org/pdf/1811.08278.pdf.

2. Study the research paper "A Survey of the Recent Architectures of Deep Convolutional Neural Networks" at https://arxiv.org/pdf/1901.06032.pdf.

3. Go through the research paper "Understanding Convolutional Neural Networks with a Mathematical Model" at https://arxiv.org/pdf/1609.04112.pdf.

4. Go through "Evaluation of Pooling Operations in Convolutional Architectures for Object Recognition" at http://ais.uni-bonn.de/papers/icann2010_maxpool.pdf.

CHAPTER 3

Image Classification Using LeNet

The journey of a thousand miles begins with one step.

—Lao Tzu

And you have taken that extraordinary step of learning Deep Learning. Deep Learning is an evolving field. From the basic Neural Networks, we have now evolved to complex architectures solving a multitude of business problems. Deep Learning powered Image Processing and computer vision capabilities are allowing us to create better cancer detection solutions, reduce pollution levels, implement surveillance systems, and improve consumer experience. Sometimes, a business problem demands a customized approach. We might design our own network to suit the business problem at hand and based on the image quality available to us. The network design will also consider the available computation power to train and execute the networks. The researchers across organizations and universities spent a good amount of time in collecting and curating the datasets, cleaning and analyzing them, designing architectures, training and testing them, and iterating to improve the performance. It takes a good amount of time and a lot of patience to make a path-breaking solution.

In the first two chapters, we have discussed the fundamentals of a Neural Network and created a Deep Learning solution using Keras and Python. From this chapter onward, we'll start discussing complex Neural

© Vaibhav Verdhan 2021
V. Verdhan, *Computer Vision Using Deep Learning*,
https://doi.org/10.1007/978-1-4842-6616-8_3

Network architectures. We will first introduce the LeNet architecture. We will go through the network design, various layers, activation functions, and so on. Then, we'll develop models for image classification use cases.

In particular, we'll cover the following topics in this chapter:

1. LeNet architecture and its variants

2. Design of the LeNet architecture

3. MNIST digit classification

4. German traffic sign classification

5. Summary

Welcome to the third chapter and all the very best!

3.1 Technical requirements

The code and datasets for the chapter are uploaded at the GitHub link `https://github.com/Apress/computer-vision-using-deep-learning/ tree/main/Chapter3` for this book. We will use the Jupyter Notebook. For this chapter, a CPU is good enough to execute the code, but if required you can use Google Colaboratory. You can refer to the reference of the book for Google Colab.

Let's proceed with the Deep Learning architectures in the next section.

3.2 Deep Learning architectures

When we discuss a Deep Learning network, there are a few components which immediately come to our mind – number of neurons, number of layers, activation functions used, loss, and so on. All these parameters play a paramount role in the design of the network and its performance. When we refer to the depth in a Neural Network, it is the number of hidden layers in the network. With the improvement in computing power, the networks got deeper and the demand for computing power also increased.

Info   While you might think that increasing the number of layers in the network will result in an increase in accuracy, that's not always the case. This is exactly what resulted in a new network called ResNet.

Using these base components, we can design our own network. Researchers and scientists across the globe have spent a huge amount of time and efforts in coming up with different Neural Network architectures. The most popular architectures are *LeNet-5, AlexNet, VGGNet, GoogLeNet, ResNet, R-CNN (Region-based CNN), YOLO (You Only Look Once), SqueezeNet, SegNet, GAN (Generative Adversarial Network),* and so on. These networks use different numbers of hidden layers, neurons, activation functions, optimization methods, and so on. Some architectures are better suited than others based on the business problem at hand.

In this chapter, we'll discuss the LeNet architecture in detail and then develop some use cases. We are starting with LeNet as it is one of the easier frameworks to understand and one of the pioneers in Deep Learning architectures. We'll also check the impact on the performance of our model with changes in various hyperparameters.

3.3 LeNet architecture

As we discussed in the last section, LeNet is the first architecture we are discussing in the book. It is one of the simpler CNN architectures. It has garnered significance because before it was invented, character recognition was a cumbersome and time-consuming process. The LeNet architecture was introduced in 1998, and it gained popularity when it was used to classify handwritten digits on bank checks in the United States.

The LeNet architecture has a few forms – *LeNet-1*, *LeNet-4*, and *LeNet-5*, which is the most cited and celebrated one. They were developed by Yann LeCun over a period of time. In the interest of space, we are examining LeNet-5 in detail, and the rest of the architectures can be understood using the same methodology.

We are starting with the basic LeNet-1 architecture in the next section.

3.4 LeNet-1 architecture

The LeNet-1 architecture is simple to understand. Let's look at the dimensions of its layers.

First layer: 28x28 input image

Second layer: Four 24x24 Convolutional Layer (5x5 size)

Third layer: Average pooling layer (2×2 size)

Fourth layer: Eight 12×12 convolutional layer (5×5 size)

Fifth layer: Average pooling layers (2×2 size)

And finally, we have the output layer.

Info   When LeNet was introduced, the researchers did not propose max pooling; instead, average pooling was used. You are advised to test the solution by using both average and max pooling.

The LeNet-1 architecture is shown in Figure 3-1.

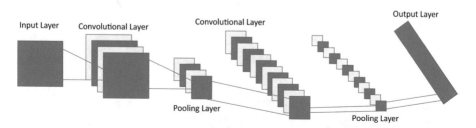

Figure 3-1. *LeNet-1 architecture is the first LeNet conceptualized. We should note how we have the first layer as a convolutional layer, followed by pooling, another convolutional layer, and a pooling layer. And finally, we have an output layer at the end*

You can see over here that we have the input layer, followed by the Convolutional Layer, then the Pooling Layer, followed by the Convolutional Layer, then the Pooling Layer, and then finally the output. The images are getting transformed during the entire network as per the configurations. We have explained in detail the function of all the layers and respective outputs while we discuss LeNet-5 in the subsequent sections.

3.5 LeNet-4 architecture

The LeNet-4 architecture is a slight improvement over LeNet-1. There is one more Fully Connected Layer and more feature maps.

First layer: 32x32 input image

Second layer: Four 24x24 Convolutional Layer (5x5 size)

Third layer: Average pooling layer (2×2 size)

Fourth layer: Sixteen 12×12 convolutional layer (5×5 size)

Fifth layer: Average pooling layers (2×2 size)

The output is fully connected to 120 neurons, which are fully connected further to 10 neurons as the final output.

The LeNet-4 architecture is shown in Figure 3-2.

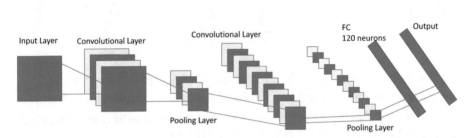

Figure 3-2. *LeNet-4 is an improvement over the LeNet-1 architecture. One more fully connected layer has been introduced in it*

For a detailed understanding of the function of all the layers, refer to the next section where we discuss LeNet-5.

3.6 LeNet-5 architecture

Between all three LeNet architectures, the most quoted architecture is LeNet-5, and it is the one which is generally used while solving the business problems.

The LeNet-5 architecture is shown in Figure 3-3. It was originally discussed in the paper "Gradient-Based Learning Applied to Document Recognition," Y. LeCun et al. The paper can be accessed at http://yann. lecun.com/exdb/publis/pdf/lecun-01a.pdf.

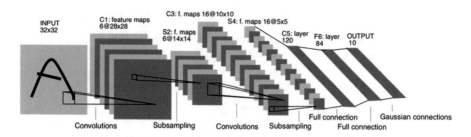

Figure 3-3. *LeNet architecture – the image has been taken from* `http://yann.lecun.com/exdb/publis/pdf/lecun-01a.pdf`

Let's discuss its layers in detail as it's the most commonly used architecture:

1. First layer: The first layer of LeNet-5 is a 32x32 input image layer. It is a grayscale image that passes through a convolutional block with six filters of size 5x5. The resulting dimensions are 28x28x1 from 32x32x1. Here, 1 represents the channel; it's 1 because it's a grayscale image. If it was RGB, it would have been three channels.

2. Second layer: The pooling layer also called the *subsampling layer* has a filter size of 2x2 and a stride of 2. Image dimensions are reduced to 14x14x6.

3. Third layer: This is again a Convolutional Layer with 16 feature maps, a size of 5x5, and a stride of 1. Note that in this layer, only 10 out of 16 feature maps are connected to 6 feature maps of the previous layer. It gives us a few clear advantages:

   a. The computation cost is lower. This is because the number of connections is reduced to 151,600 from 240,000.

   b. The total number of training parameters for this layer is 1516 instead of 2400.

   c. It also breaks the symmetry of the architecture, and hence the learning in the network is better.

4. Fourth layer: It is a pooling layer with a filter size of 2x2 and a stride of 2 with output as 5x5x16.

5. Fifth layer: It is a Fully Connected Convolutional layer with 120 feature maps and size being 1x1 each. Each of the 120 units is connected to 400 nodes in the previous layer.

6. Sixth layer: It is a Fully Connected layer with 84 units.

7. Finally, the output layer is a softmax layer with ten possible values corresponding to each digit.

A summary of the LeNet-5 architecture is shown in Table 3-1.

Table 3-1. *Summary of the entire LeNet architecture*

Layer	Operation	Feature Map	Input Size	Kernel Size	Stride	Activation function
Input		1	32x32			
1	Convolution	6	28x28	5x2	1	tanh
2	Average Pooling	6	14x14	2x2	2	tanh
3	Convolution	16	10x10	5x2	1	tanh
4	Average Pooling	16	5x5	2x2	2	tanh
5	Convolution	120	1x1	5x2	1	tanh
6	Fully Connected	-	84			tanh
Output	Fully Connected	-	10			softmax

LeNet is a small and very easy architecture to understand. Yet, it is large and mature enough to generate good results. It can be executed on a CPU too. At the same time, it will be a good idea to test the solution with different architectures and test the accuracy to choose the best one.

We have a boosted LeNet architecture which is being discussed next.

3.7 Boosted LeNet-4 architecture

Boosting is an ensemble technique that combines weak learners into strong ones by constantly improving from the previous iteration. In Boosted LeNet-4, the outputs of the architectures are added, and the one with the highest value is the predicted class.

The Boosted LeNet-4 architecture is shown in Figure 3-4.

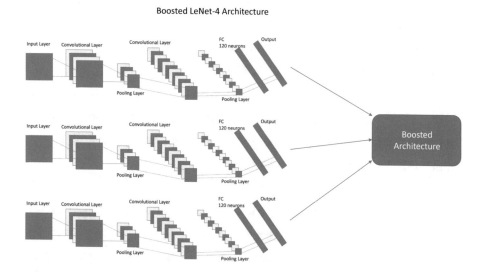

Figure 3-4. *Boosted LeNet-4 architecture combines weak learners to make an improvement. The final output is much more accurate and robust*

In the network architecture depicted earlier, we can see how the weak learners are combined to make a strong predictive solution.

LeNet is the first of the few architectures which became popular and were used to solve Deep Learning problems. With more progress and research, we have developed advanced algorithms, but still LeNet retains a special place.

It is time for us to create the first solution using the LeNet architecture.

3.8 Creating image classification models using LeNet

Now that we have understood the LeNet architecture, it is time to develop actual use cases with it. We are going to develop two use cases using the LeNet architecture. LeNet is a simple architecture so the code can be compiled on your CPU itself. We are making slight adjustments to the architecture in terms of the activation functions using the Max Pooling function instead of Average Pooling and so on.

Info   Max pooling extracts the important features as compared to average pooling. Average pooling smooths the image, and hence sharp features might not be identified.

Before we start with the code, there is a small setting we should be aware of. The position of the channels in the tensor decides how we should reshape our data. This can be observed in step 8 of the following case study.

Each image can be represented by height, width, and the number of channels or number of channels, height, and width. If channels are at the first position of the input array, we reshape using the channels_first condition. It means that channels are in the first position in a tensor (n-dimensional array). And vice versa is true for channels_last.

3.9 MNIST classification using LeNet

This use case is a continuation of the MNIST dataset we used in the previous chapter. The code is checked in at GitHub link given at the start of the chapter

1. First, import all the required libraries.

```
import keras
from keras.optimizers import SGD
from sklearn.preprocessing import
LabelBinarizer from sklearn.model_selection
import train_test_split from sklearn.metrics
import classification_report from sklearn
import datasets
from keras import backend as K
import matplotlib.pyplot as plt
import numpy as np
```

2. Next, we import the dataset and then we import a series of layers from Keras.

```
from keras.datasets import mnist ## Data set is
imported here
from keras.models import Sequential
from keras.layers.convolutional import Conv2D
from keras.layers.convolutional import
MaxPooling2D
from keras.layers.core import Activation
from keras.layers.core import Flatten
from keras.layers.core import Dense
from keras import backend as K
```

3. Define the hyperparameters. This step is similar to
    the one in the previous chapter where we developed
    the MNIST and dog/cat classification.

```
image_rows, image_cols = 28, 28
batch_size = 256
num_classes = 10
epochs = 10
```

4. Load the dataset now. MNIST is the dataset that is
    added by default in the library.

```
(x_train, y_train), (x_test, y_test) =
mnist.load_data()
```

5. Convert the image data to float and then normalize it.

```
x_train = x_train.astype('float32')
x_test = x_test.astype('float32') x_train /= 255
x_test /= 255
```

6. Let's print the shape of our train and test datasets.

```
print('x_train shape:', x_train.shape)
print(x_train.shape[0], 'train samples')
print(x_test.shape[0], 'test samples')
```

7. In the next block of code, we convert our variables
    into one-hot encoding. We use Keras's to_
    categorical method for it.

```
y_train = keras.utils.to_categorical(y_train,
num_classes)
y_test = keras.utils.to_categorical(y_test,
num_classes)
```

Tip   We are using print statements to analyze the output at each of the steps. It allows us to debug at a later stage if required.

---

8.   Let's reshape our data accordingly.

```
if K.image_data_format() == 'channels_first':
    x_train = x_train.reshape(x_train.shape[0],
    1, image_rows, image_cols)
    x_test = x_test.reshape(x_test.shape[0], 1,
    image_rows, image_cols)
    input_shape = (1, image_rows, image_cols)
else:
    x_train = x_train.reshape(x_train.shape[0],
    image_rows, image_cols, 1)
    x_test = x_test.reshape(x_test.shape[0],
    image_rows, image_cols, 1)
    input_shape = (image_rows, image_cols, 1)
```

It's time to create our model!

9.   Start with adding a sequential layer, followed by a Convolutional Layer and the Max Pooling layer.

```
model = Sequential()
model.add(Conv2D(20, (5, 5),
padding="same",input_shape=input_shape))
model.add(Activation("relu")) model.
add(MaxPooling2D(pool_size=(2, 2),
strides=(2, 2)))
```

10.   We are now going to add multiple layers of the Convolutional layer, Max Pooling layers, and layers to flatten the data.

```
model.add(Conv2D(50, (5, 5), padding="same"))
model.add(Activation("relu")) model.
add(MaxPooling2D(pool_size=(2, 2),
strides=(2, 2)))
model.add(Flatten()) model.add(Dense(500))
model.add(Activation("relu"))
```

11.   We add a Dense Layer followed by the softmax layer. Softmax is used for classification models. After that, we compile our model.

```
model.add(Dense(num_classes)) model.
add(Activation("softmax"))
model.compile(loss=keras.losses.categorical_
crossentropy, optimizer=keras.optimizers.
Adadelta(), metrics=['accuracy'])
```

The model is ready to be trained and fit.

12.   We can see the impact per epoch on accuracy and loss. We encourage you to try with different variations of hyperparameters like epoch and batch size. Depending on the hyperparameters, the network will take time to process.

```
theLeNetModel = model.fit(x_train, y_train,
batch_size=batch_size,
epochs=epochs,
verbose=1, validation_data=(x_test, y_test))
```

Here, we can analyze how the loss and accuracy vary with each epoch.

```
Train on 60000 samples, validate on 10000 samples
Epoch 1/10
60000/60000 [==============================] - 36s 607us/step - loss: 0.2736 - acc: 0.9127 - val_loss: 0.1051 - val_a
cc: 0.9649
Epoch 2/10
60000/60000 [==============================] - 37s 622us/step - loss: 0.0590 - acc: 0.9813 - val_loss: 0.0490 - val_a
cc: 0.9835
Epoch 3/10
60000/60000 [==============================] - 37s 614us/step - loss: 0.0387 - acc: 0.9879 - val_loss: 0.0939 - val_a
cc: 0.9671
Epoch 4/10
60000/60000 [==============================] - 37s 625us/step - loss: 0.0285 - acc: 0.9910 - val_loss: 0.0267 - val_a
cc: 0.9905
Epoch 5/10
60000/60000 [==============================] - 37s 615us/step - loss: 0.0215 - acc: 0.9933 - val_loss: 0.0305 - val_a
cc: 0.9896
Epoch 6/10
60000/60000 [==============================] - 37s 614us/step - loss: 0.0164 - acc: 0.9949 - val_loss: 0.0228 - val_a
cc: 0.9920
Epoch 7/10
60000/60000 [==============================] - 37s 614us/step - loss: 0.0136 - acc: 0.9955 - val_loss: 0.0236 - val_a
cc: 0.9918
Epoch 8/10
60000/60000 [==============================] - 37s 616us/step - loss: 0.0106 - acc: 0.9969 - val_loss: 0.0279 - val_a
cc: 0.9909
Epoch 9/10
60000/60000 [==============================] - 37s 617us/step - loss: 0.0082 - acc: 0.9976 - val_loss: 0.0246 - val_a
cc: 0.9917
Epoch 10/10
60000/60000 [==============================] - 37s 620us/step - loss: 0.0062 - acc: 0.9983 - val_loss: 0.0316 - val_a
cc: 0.9907
```

After ten epochs, the validation accuracy is 99.07%.

Now, let us visualize the results.

13. We will be plotting the training and testing accuracy in the next code block.

```
import matplotlib.pyplot as plt
f, ax = plt.subplots()
ax.plot([None] + theLeNetModel.history['acc'], 'o-')
ax.plot([None] + theLeNetModel.history['val_acc'], 'x-')
ax.legend(['Train acc', 'Validation acc'], loc = 0)
ax.set_title('Training/Validation acc per Epoch')
ax.set_xlabel('Epoch')
ax.set_ylabel('acc')
```

In the graph in Figure 3-5, we can see that with each subsequent epoch, the respective accuracy parameters for both training and validation continue to increase. After epoch 7/8, the accuracy stabilizes. We can test this with different values of hyperparameters.

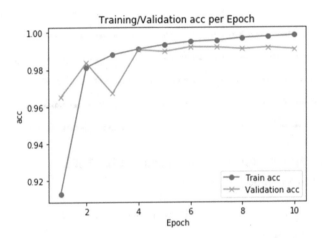

Figure 3-5. *Training and validation accuracy are shown here. After epoch 7/8, the accuracy has stabilized*

14.   Let's analyze the loss:

```
import matplotlib.pyplot as plt f,
ax = plt.subplots()
ax.plot([None] + theLeNetModel.history['loss'], 'o-')
ax.plot([None] + theLeNetModel.history['val_loss'], 'x-')
ax.legend(['Train loss', 'Validation loss'], loc = 0)
ax.set_title('Training/Validation loss per Epoch')
ax.set_xlabel('Epoch')
ax.set_ylabel('acc')
```

In the graph in Figure 3-6, we can see that with each subsequent epoch, the respective loss measures for both training and validation continue to decrease. After epoch 7/8, the accuracy stabilizes. We can test this with different values of hyperparameters.

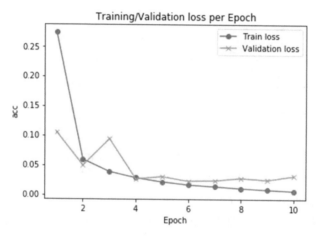

Figure 3-6. *Training and validation loss are shown here. After 7/8 epochs, the loss has stabilized and not much reductions are being observed*

Great! Now we have a working LeNet model to classify the images.

In this exercise, we trained an image classification model using the LeNet-5 architecture.

Info   Use Google Colaboratory if you face any challenge with computation efficiency.

3.10 German traffic sign identification using LeNet

The second use case is the German traffic sign identification. It can be used in autonomous driving solutions.

In this use case, we are going to build a Deep Learning model using the LeNet-5 architecture.

1. We are going to follow a similar process throughout the book which is importing the libraries first.

```
import keras
from keras.optimizers import SGD
from sklearn.preprocessing import
LabelBinarizer
from sklearn.model_selection import train_test_split
from sklearn.metrics import classification_report
from sklearn import datasets
from keras import backend as K
import matplotlib.pyplot as plt
import numpy as np
```

2. Import the Keras libraries along with all the packages required to create plots.

```
from keras.models import Sequential
from keras.layers.convolutional import Conv2D
from keras.layers.convolutional import
MaxPooling2D
from keras.layers.core import Activation
from keras.layers.core import Flatten
from keras.layers.core import Dense
from keras import backend as K
```

3. Then import general libraries like numpy,
    matplotlib, os, OpenCV, and so on.

```
import glob
import pandas as pd
import matplotlib
import matplotlib.pyplot as plt
import random
import matplotlib.image as mpimg
import cv2
import os
from sklearn.model_selection import train_test_
split
from sklearn.metrics import confusion_matrix
from sklearn.utils import shuffle
import warnings
from skimage import exposure
# Load pickled data
import pickle
%matplotlib inline matplotlib.style.
use('ggplot')
%config InlineBackend.figure_format = 'retina'
```

4. The dataset is provided as a pickle file and is saved
    as a train.p and test.p files. The dataset can be
    downloaded from Kaggle at www.kaggle.com/
    meowmeowmeowmeowmeow/gtsrb-german-traffic-
    sign.

```
training_file = "train.p"
testing_file = "test.p"
```

5. Open the files and save the data inside the train and
    test variables.

```
with open(training_file, mode='rb') as f: train
= pickle.load(f)
with open(testing_file, mode='rb') as f: test =
pickle.load(f)
```

6. Divide the dataset into test and train. We've taken a
    test size of 4000 here, but you are free to try different
    test sizes.

```
X, y = train['features'], train['labels']
x_train, x_valid, y_train, y_valid = train_
test_split(X, y, stratify=y,
test_size=4000, random_state=0)
x_test,y_test=test['features'],test['labels']
```

7. Let's have a look at some of the sample image files
    here. We have used the random function to select
    random images; thus, don't worry if your output is
    not the same as ours.

```
figure, axiss = plt.subplots(2,5, figsize=(15, 4))
figure.subplots_adjust(hspace = .2, wspace=.001)
axiss = axiss.ravel()
for i in range(10):
    index = random.randint(0, len(x_train))
    image = x_train[index]
    axiss[i].axis('off')
    axiss[i].imshow(image)
    axiss[i].set_title( y_train[index])
```

Here's the output as shown in Figure 3-7.

Figure 3-7. *Some examples of the German traffic sign classification dataset are shown here*

8. Next, let's choose our hyperparameters. The number of distinct classes is 43. We have taken ten epochs to start with, but we encourage you to check the performance with different values of epochs. The same is true for batch size too.

```
image_rows, image_cols = 32, 32
batch_size = 256
num_classes = 43
epochs = 10
```

9. Now, we'll perform some exploratory data analysis. This is done to see how our image dataset looks and what are the frequency distributions of various classes in a histogram.

```
histogram, the_bins = np.histogram(y_train,
bins=num_classes) the_width = 0.7 * (the_
bins[1] - the_bins[0])
```

```
center = (the_bins[:-1] + the_bins[1:]) / 2
plt.bar(center, histogram, align='center',
width=the_width) plt.show()
```

The output is shown in Figure 3-8. We can observe that there is a difference in the number of examples of classes. A few classes are very well represented, while some are not. In a real-world solution, we would wish to have a balanced dataset. We are discussing more on it in Chapter 8 of the book.

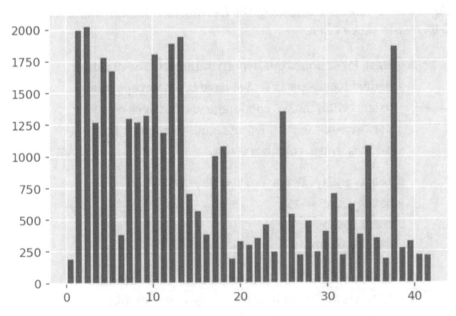

Figure 3-8. *Frequency distribution of various classes. Some classes have more examples, while some do not have much representation. Ideally, we should collect more data for less-represented classes*

10. Now, let us check how the distribution is across the
     different classes. It is a regular histogram function
     from the NumPy library.

```
train_hist, train_bins = np.histogram(y_train,
bins=num_classes)
test_hist, test_bins = np.histogram(y_test,
bins=num_classes)
train_width = 0.7 * (train_bins[1] - train_ bins[0])
train_center = (train_bins[:-1] + train_bins[1:]) / 2
test_width = 0.7 * (test_ bins[1] - test_bins[0])
test_center = (test_ bins[:-1] + test_bins[1:]) / 2
```

11. Now, plot the histograms; the color is set to red and
     green for train and test datasets, respectively.

```
plt.bar(train_center, train_hist,
align='center', color='red', width=train_width)
plt.bar(test_center, test_hist, align='center',
color='green', width=test_width)
plt.show()
```

Here's the output as shown in Figure 3-9.

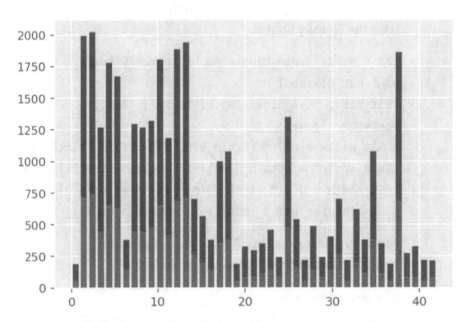

Figure 3-9. *Frequency distribution of various classes and distributed between train and test datasets. The train is shown in red color, while the test is depicted in green color*

Let's analyze the distribution here; look at the difference in the proportion of train vs. test in the preceding histogram.

12. Convert the image data to float and then normalize it.

```
x_train = x_train.astype('float32')
x_test = x_test.astype('float32')
x_train /= 255
x_test /= 255
print('x_train shape:', x_train.shape)
print(x_ train.shape[0], 'train samples')
print(x_test. shape[0], 'test samples')
```

So, we have 35,209 training data points and 12,630 testing ones. In the next step, convert class vectors to binary class matrices. This is similar to the steps in the last example where we developed the MNIST classification.

```
y_train = keras.utils.to_categorical(y_train, num_classes)
y_test = keras.utils.to_categorical(y_test, num_classes)
```

The following code block is the same as the one described in the MNIST classification developed earlier. Here, channels_first means that channels are at the first position in the array. And we are changing the input_shape depending on the position of channels_first.

```
if K.image_data_format() == 'channels_first':
    input_shape = (1, image_rows, image_cols)
else:
    input_shape = (image_rows, image_cols, 1)
```

Let us start creating the Neural Network Architecture now. The steps are similar to the previous use case.

13. Add a sequential layer followed by a Convolutional layer.

```
model = Sequential() model.add(Conv2D(16,(3,3),
input_shape=(32,32,3)))
```

14. Add the Pooling layer followed by Convolutional layers and so on.

```
model.add(Activation("relu")) model.
add(MaxPooling2D(pool_size=(2, 2),
strides=(2, 2)))
```

```
model.add(Conv2D(50, (5, 5), padding="same"))
model.add(Activation("relu")) model.
add(MaxPooling2D(pool_size=(2, 2),
strides=(2, 2)))
model.add(Flatten()) model.add(Dense(500))
model.add(Activation("relu"))
model.add(Dense(num_classes)) model.
add(Activation("softmax"))
```

15. Let us print the model summary.

```
model.summary()
```

Here's the output.

Layer (type)	Output Shape	Param #
conv2d_15 (Conv2D)	(None, 30, 30, 16)	448
activation_13 (Activation)	(None, 30, 30, 16)	0
max_pooling2d_7 (MaxPooling2	(None, 15, 15, 16)	0
conv2d_16 (Conv2D)	(None, 15, 15, 50)	20050
activation_14 (Activation)	(None, 15, 15, 50)	0
max_pooling2d_8 (MaxPooling2	(None, 7, 7, 50)	0
flatten_4 (Flatten)	(None, 2450)	0
dense_7 (Dense)	(None, 500)	1225500
activation_15 (Activation)	(None, 500)	0
dense_8 (Dense)	(None, 43)	21543
activation_16 (Activation)	(None, 43)	0

```
Total params: 1,267,541
Trainable params: 1,267,541
Non-trainable params: 0
```

16. The model is ready to be compiled; let's train it.

```
model.compile(loss=keras.losses.categorical_
crossentropy, optimizer=keras.optimizers.
Adadelta(), metrics=['accuracy'])
theLeNetModel = model.fit(x_train, y_train,
batch_size=batch_size,
epochs=epochs,
verbose=1,
validation_data=(x_test, y_test))
```

Here's the output as shown in Figure 3-10.

```
WARNING:tensorflow:From /Users/vaibhavverdhan/anaconda3/lib/python3.6/site-packages/tensorflow/python/ops/math_ops.p
y:3066: to_int32 (from tensorflow.python.ops.math_ops) is deprecated and will be removed in a future version.
Instructions for updating:
Use tf.cast instead.
Train on 35209 samples, validate on 12630 samples
Epoch 1/10
35209/35209 [==============================] - 22s 632us/step - loss: 2.2025 - acc: 0.3971 - val_loss: 1.4474 - val_a
cc: 0.5604
Epoch 2/10
35209/35209 [==============================] - 22s 631us/step - loss: 0.5801 - acc: 0.8291 - val_loss: 0.6247 - val_a
cc: 0.8179
Epoch 3/10
35209/35209 [==============================] - 22s 629us/step - loss: 0.1937 - acc: 0.9501 - val_loss: 0.4696 - val_a
cc: 0.8833
Epoch 4/10
35209/35209 [==============================] - 22s 623us/step - loss: 0.0956 - acc: 0.9770 - val_loss: 0.4750 - val_a
cc: 0.8850
Epoch 5/10
35209/35209 [==============================] - 23s 651us/step - loss: 0.0564 - acc: 0.9876 - val_loss: 0.5317 - val_a
cc: 0.8864
Epoch 6/10
35209/35209 [==============================] - 23s 642us/step - loss: 0.0364 - acc: 0.9925 - val_loss: 0.4336 - val_a
cc: 0.9140
Epoch 7/10
35209/35209 [==============================] - 22s 630us/step - loss: 0.0251 - acc: 0.9953 - val_loss: 0.4621 - val_a
cc: 0.9138
Epoch 8/10
35209/35209 [==============================] - 22s 631us/step - loss: 0.0186 - acc: 0.9964 - val_loss: 0.4819 - val_a
cc: 0.9117
Epoch 9/10
35209/35209 [==============================] - 22s 628us/step - loss: 0.0121 - acc: 0.9981 - val_loss: 0.5061 - val_a
cc: 0.9124
Epoch 10/10
35209/35209 [==============================] - 22s 619us/step - loss: 0.0112 - acc: 0.9983 - val_loss: 0.5421 - val_a
cc: 0.9116
```

Figure 3-10. *The accuracy and loss movement with respect to each epoch. We should note how the accuracy has improved from the first epoch to the last one*

After ten epochs, the validation accuracy is 91.16%.

Let us visualize the results now.

17. We will first plot the training and testing accuracy
     for the network.

```
import matplotlib.pyplot as plt
f, ax = plt.subplots()
ax.plot([None] + theLeNetModel.history['acc'], 'o-')
ax.plot([None] + theLeNetModel. history['val_acc'], 'x-')
ax.legend(['Train acc', 'Validation acc'], loc = 0)
ax.set_ title('Training/Validation acc per Epoch')
ax.set_xlabel('Epoch')
ax.set_ylabel('acc')
```

Here's the resulting plot as shown in Figure 3-11.

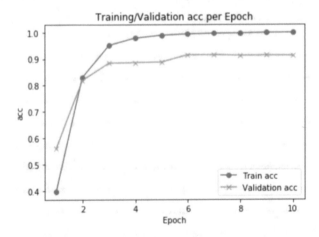

Figure 3-11. *Training and validation accuracy are shown here. After epoch 5/6, the accuracy has stabilized*

18. Let's plot the loss for training and testing data.

```
import matplotlib.pyplot as plt
f, ax = plt.subplots()
ax.plot([None] + theLeNetModel.history['loss'], 'o-')
ax.plot([None] + theLeNetModel. history['val_loss'], 'x-')
ax.legend(['Train loss', 'Validation loss'], loc = 0)
ax.set_ title('Training/Validation loss per Epoch')
ax.set_xlabel('Epoch')
ax.set_ylabel('acc')
```

The resulting plot can be seen in Figure 3-12.

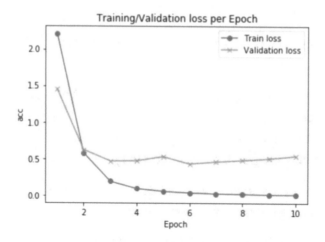

Figure 3-12. *Training and validation loss are shown here. After 5/6 epochs, the loss has stabilized and not much reductions are being observed*

The accuracy and loss function plots are generated to measure the performance of the model. The plots are similar to the ones developed in the MNIST classification model.

Info   All the model's performance parameters are inside
theLeNetModel.model or theLeNetModel.model.metrics.

In this example, we are taking one additional step
and creating the Confusion Matrix for the prediction
too. For this, we have to first make the predictions
over the test set and then compare the predictions
with the actual labels of the images.

19. Make the prediction using the predict function.

```
predictions = theLeNetModel.model.predict
(x_test)
```

20. Now, let us create the Confusion Matrix. It is
available in the scikit-learn library.

```
from sklearn.metrics import confusion_matrix
import numpy as np
confusion = confusion_matrix(y_test,
np.argmax(predictions,axis=1))
```

21. Let us now create a variable called cm which is
nothing but the confusion matrix.

Feel free to print it and analyze the results.

```
cm = confusion_matrix(y_test,
np.argmax(predictions,axis=1))
```

22. Now let us start the visualization for the Confusion
Matrix. Seaborn is another library along with
matplotlib which is used for visualization.

```
import seaborn as sn
df_cm = pd.DataFrame(cm, columns=np.unique
(y_test), index = np.unique(y_test))
```

```
df_cm.index.name = 'Actual'
df_cm.columns.name = 'Predicted'
plt.figure(figsize = (10,7))
sn.set(font_scale=1.4)#for label size
sn.heatmap(df_cm, cmap="Blues",
annot=True,annot_kws={"size": 16})# font size
```

The output is shown as follows. Due to the number of dimensions, the Confusion Matrix is not clearly visible in Figure 3-13, so let's make it a little better in the next code block.

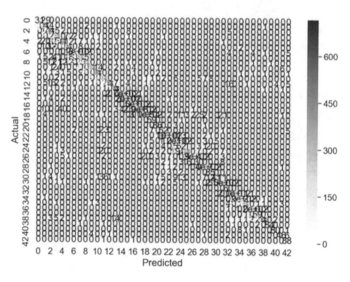

Figure 3-13. *Confusion matrix is shown, but due to the number of dimensions, the output is not very clear which we are improving in the next figure*

23.   Here, we are plotting the Confusion Matrix again.
Please note that we have defined a function plot_
confusion_matrix which takes a confusion matrix
as the input parameter. Then we are using the
regular matplotlib library and its functions to plot
the Confusion Matrix. You can use this function for
other solutions too.

```
def plot_confusion_matrix(cm):
cm = [row/sum(row) for row in cm]
fig = plt.figure(figsize=(10, 10))
ax = fig.add_subplot(111)
cax = ax.matshow(cm, cmap=plt.cm.Oranges) fig.
colorbar(cax)
plt.title('Confusion Matrix') plt.
xlabel('Predicted Class IDs') plt.ylabel('True
Class IDs')
plt.show()
    plot_confusion_matrix(cm)
```

Here's the plot that shows the confusion matrix (Figure 3-14).

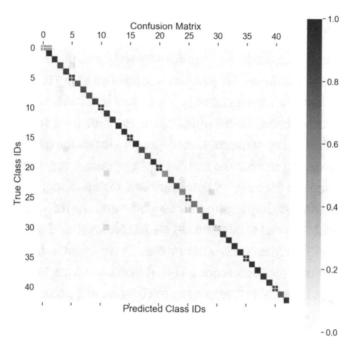

Figure 3-14. *Confusion matrix generated for all the classes. For a few classes, the results are not very good. It is advisable to scout for the misclassifications and analyze the reason*

We can see over here that for some classes we do have great results. You are advised to analyze the results and iterate with hyperparameters to see the impact. The observations which have misclassifications should be analyzed to find out the reason. For example, in the case of digit classification, an algorithm might become confused between 1 and 7. Hence, once we have tested the model, we should look for the misclassifications done and find out the reason. A potential solution is to remove the confusing images from the training dataset. Improving the quality of the images and increasing the quantity of the misclassified classes can also help in tackling the issue.

With this, we have completed the two case studies on image classification using LeNet. We are coming to the end of the chapter. You can proceed to the summary now.

3.11 Summary

Neural Network architectures are quite interesting and powerful solutions to computer vision problems. They allow us to train on a very large dataset and are useful to identify images correctly. This capability can be used for a very large variety of problems across domains. At the same time, it is imperative to note that the quality of the solution depends a lot on the quality of the training dataset. Remember the famous saying, garbage in garbage out.

We studied the concepts of convolutional, max pooling, padding, and so on in the last chapters and developed solutions using CNN. This chapter marks the start of customized Neural Network architectures. These architectures differ from each other by their design, that is, the number of layers, activation functions, strides, kernel size, and so on. More often, we test three of four distinct architectures to compare the accuracies.

In this chapter, we discussed LeNet architectures and focused on LeNet-5. We developed two use cases with end-to-end implementation right from data loading to designing of the network and testing the accuracy.

In the next chapter, we'll study another popular architecture called VGGNet.

You should be able to answer the questions in the exercise now!

REVIEW EXERCISES

1. What is the difference between different versions of LeNet?

2. How can we measure accuracy distribution with epoch?

3. We have discussed two use cases in the chapter. Iterate the same solution with different values of hyperparameters. Create a loss function and accuracy distribution for the use cases done in the last chapter.

4. Take the dataset used in the last chapter and test with LeNet-5 to compare the results.

5. Download the Image Scene classification dataset from `www.kaggle.com/puneet6060/intel-image-classification/version/2`. Execute the code used in the German traffic classification dataset for this dataset.

6. Download the Linnaeus 5 dataset from `http://chaladze.com/l5/`. It contains five classes – berry, bird, dog, flower, and other. Use this dataset to create a CNN-based solution.

3.11.1 Further readings

1. Go through the paper "Convolutional Neural Network for 3D object recognition using volumetric representation" at `https://drive.google.com/drive/folders/1-5V1vj88-ANdRQJ5PpcAQkErvG7lqzxs`.

2. Go through the paper for Alzheimer's disease classification using CNN at `https://arxiv.org/abs/1603.08631`.

CHAPTER 4

VGGNet and AlexNet Networks

Once we accept our limits, we go beyond them.

—Albert Einstein

After a certain point, even an extremely complex solution ceases to improve. And then we should improve the design of the solution. We go back to the drawing board and put our heads together to improve the capabilities. With more options available, we can iterate and test multiple solutions. And then based on the business problem at hand, the best solution will be chosen and implemented. We follow the same principle in Deep Learning architectures. We work on a network architecture, improve it, and make it more robust, accurate, and efficient. The selection of the Neural Network architectures is based on the testing done of various architectures.

In the last chapter, we started with the LeNet Deep Learning architecture. We went through the network architecture and developed use cases using it. In this chapter, we are going to discuss VGG and AlexNet Neural Network architectures and develop a complex multiclass classification capability. We will also compare the performance of the two architectures. Along with this, we will discuss how we can use a checkpoint

© Vaibhav Verdhan 2021
V. Verdhan, *Computer Vision Using Deep Learning*,
https://doi.org/10.1007/978-1-4842-6616-8_4

while training a Deep Learning model. There is one common error which we face while generating the Confusion Matrix; we will understand the reason for that error and how to rectify it.

We will cover the following topics in this chapter:

1.   AlexNet architecture

2.   VGG16 architecture

3.   Difference between VGG16 and VGG19

4.   CIFAR-10 case study using AlexNet

5.   CIFAR-10 case study using VGG16

Welcome to the fourth chapter and all the very best!

4.1 Technical requirements

The code and datasets for the chapter are uploaded at the GitHub link `https://github.com/Apress/computer-vision-using-deep-learning/tree/main/Chapter4` for this book. We will use the Jupyter Notebook. For this chapter, a CPU is good enough to execute the code, but if required you can use Google Colaboratory. You can refer to the reference of the book, if you are not able to set up the Google Colab yourself.

Let's proceed with the Deep Learning architectures in the next section.

4.2 AlexNet and VGG Neural Networks

AlexNet was introduced in 2012 and immediately became everyone's favorite for Image and Object Classification purposes. It also went on to win the ImageNet Large-Scale Visual Recognition Challenge (ILSVRC). Subsequently, VGG came into existence in 2014, and its accuracy turned out to be better than AlexNet. It does not mean that AlexNet is not an efficient network, it just means that VGG had better accuracy.

Now let's understand both of these architectures in detail. We start with AlexNet as the first architecture.

4.3 What is AlexNet Neural Network?

AlexNet was proposed by Alex Krizhevsky, Ilya Sutskever, and Geoffrey E. Hinton. The original paper can be accessed at https://papers.nips. cc/paper/4824-imagenet-classification-with-deep-convolutional-neural-networks.pdf.

The AlexNet architecture looks like Figure 4-1. This is the original image from the abovementioned paper.

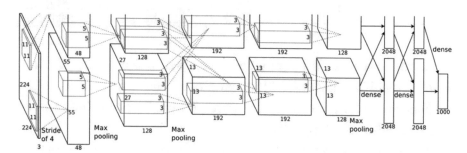

Figure 4-1. *The complete AlexNet architecture (image has been taken from https://papers.nips.cc/paper/4824-imagenet-classification-with-deep-convolutional-neural-networks.pdf)*

We can now explore the various layers in more detail. Table 4-1 gives the description of all the layers of the network.

Table 4-1. *Each of the layers of the network and the corresponding input parameters, the channel size, strides, and the activation functions*

Layer	Operation	Feature Map	Input Size	Kernel Size	Stride	Activation function
Input	Image	1	227x227x3			
1	Convolution	96	55x55x96	11x11	4	ReLU
	Max Pooling	96	27x27x96	3x3	2	ReLU
1	Convolution	256	27x27x256	5x5	1	ReLU
	Max Pooling	256	13x13x256	3x3	2	ReLU
3	Convolution	384	13x13x384	3x3	1	ReLU
4	Convolution	384	13x13x384	3x3	1	ReLU
5	Convolution	256	13x13x256	3x3	1	ReLU
	Max Pooling	256	6x6x256	3x3	2	ReLU
6	Fully Connected		9216			ReLU
7	Fully Connected		4096			ReLU
8	Fully Connected		4096			ReLU
	Output		1000			Softmax

As we can see, the first layer is an input image of size 227x227x3. It is passed through the first Convolution layer of 96 feature maps, stride of 4, and filter size of 11x11, with ReLU as the activation function. The output image is of 55x55x96 dimensions.

It is followed by a Max Pooling layer of filter size 3x3 and stride of 2 with an output image of 27x27x96 dimensions. You can continue the analysis of each layer in this fashion. It is imperative that each layer and its respective function is understood completely.

AlexNet has 60 million parameters and 650K neurons. As we can observe, in total there are eight layers. The first five layers are for performing convolutional operations. The last three layers are fully connected one. In the convolutional layers, a few have the following layer as a max pool layer. ReLU nonlinearity was used in AlexNet which showed improved training performance and faster training of the network as compared to tanh and sigmoid activations. The inventors used data augmentation and dropout layers to fight overfitting in the network.

Now let's understand the VGG architecture, and then we will develop use cases using both AlexNet and VGG.

4.4 What is VGG Neural Network?

VGGNet is a CNN architecture proposed by Karen Simonyan and Andrew Zisserman at the University of Oxford. VGG is Visual Geometry Group. You can access the original paper at https://arxiv.org/pdf/1409.1556.pdf.

It was introduced in 2014 and performed well in the ImageNet Large Scale Visual Recognition Challenge (ILSVRC). It is one of the most popular Deep Learning architectures because of its simplicity (which we will study in the following sections). Often, people criticize the size of the network as it requires more computation power and more time. But the network is a very robust solution and is referred to as one of the standard solutions for computer vision solutions.

There are two forms of the VGG Neural Network model: *VGG16* and *VGG19*. Let's study VGG16 in detail, and then we will examine how VGG19 is different from VGG16.

4.5 VGG16 architecture

VGG is a simple network to understand because of the following reasons:

1. It uses only 3x3 convolution and 2x2 pooling throughout the network.

2. The convolutional layers use a very small kernel size (3x3).

3. There are 1x1 convolutions to linearly transform the input.

4. The stride is 1 pixel, and it helps to preserve the spatial resolution.

5. ReLU is used throughout all the hidden layers.

6. There are three Fully Connected layers with the first two layers having 4096 channels and the last one having 1000 channels. And finally we have a softmax layer.

In Figure 4-2, we can see the respective configurations with the descriptions of each layer.

ConvNet Configuration					
A	A-LRN	B	C	D	E
11 weight layers	11 weight layers	13 weight layers	16 weight layers	16 weight layers	19 weight layers
input (224 × 224 RGB image)					
conv3-64	conv3-64 **LRN**	conv3-64 **conv3-64**	conv3-64 conv3-64	conv3-64 conv3-64	conv3-64 conv3-64
maxpool					
conv3-128	conv3-128	conv3-128 **conv3-128**	conv3-128 conv3-128	conv3-128 conv3-128	conv3-128 conv3-128
maxpool					
conv3-256 conv3-256	conv3-256 conv3-256	conv3-256 conv3-256	conv3-256 conv3-256 **conv1-256**	conv3-256 conv3-256 **conv3-256**	conv3-256 conv3-256 conv3-256 **conv3-256**
maxpool					
conv3-512 conv3-512	conv3-512 conv3-512	conv3-512 conv3-512	conv3-512 conv3-512 **conv1-512**	conv3-512 conv3-512 **conv3-512**	conv3-512 conv3-512 conv3-512 **conv3-512**
maxpool					
conv3-512 conv3-512	conv3-512 conv3-512	conv3-512 conv3-512	conv3-512 conv3-512 **conv1-512**	conv3-512 conv3-512 **conv3-512**	conv3-512 conv3-512 conv3-512 **conv3-512**
maxpool					
FC-4096					
FC-4096					
FC-1000					
soft-max					

Network	A,A-LRN	B	C	D	E
Number of parameters	133	133	134	138	144

Figure 4-2. *VGG simple network*

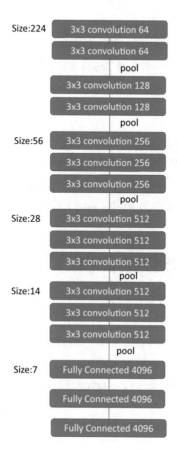

Figure 4-2. *(continued)*

Note that it utilizes only 3x3 conv layers and 2x2 pooling layers throughout the network. The figure on the left has been taken from the original paper cited earlier. The depth of the configuration increases from the left (A) to the right (E) as more layers are added. The conv layer parameters are denoted as "conv (receptive field size) – (number of channels)." The ReLU activation function is not shown for brevity.

Note   LRN (Local Response Normalization) is not used since there was no visible improvement in the accuracy despite the increase in training time.

VGG16 is quite a popular network. Owing to its simplicity, it serves as a benchmark to measure the performance for many complex image classification problems. VGG19 is slightly more complex than VGG16. The difference between the two is being studied next.

4.6 Difference between VGG16 and VGG19

Table 4-2 lists the primary differences between VGG16 and VGG19. Generally, VGG16 is mostly used and is more popular. It is due to the fact that in the general business world, we do *not* classify beyond eight to ten classes for a problem. Moreover, getting a true representative and balanced data is not achieved. Hence, in practice, VGG16 is mostly used.

Table 4-2. *The prime differences between VGG16 and VGG19*

VGG-16	VGG-19
Contains 16 layers	Contains 19 layers
Size in terms of FC layers is 533 MB	Size in terms of FC layers is 574 MB
Lighter model	Larger and deeper network
Preferred for small datasets	Can be used for richer categories as high as 1000 classes

We are now going to develop the use cases on the CIFAR-10 dataset using both AlexNet and VGG16. CIFAR-10 is an open source dataset.

4.7 Developing solutions using AlexNet and VGG

We are going to use the CIFAR dataset for creating solutions using AlexNet and VGGNet. The CIFAR dataset can be accessed at www.cs.toronto. edu/~kriz/cifar.html.

According to the source of the dataset:

The CIFAR-10 dataset consists of 60000 32x32 color images in 10 classes, with 6000 images per class. There are 50000 training images and 10000 test images. The dataset is divided into five training batches and one test batch, each with 10000 images. The test batch contains exactly 1000 randomly-selected images from each class. The training batches contain the remaining images in random order, but some training batches may contain more images from one class than another. Between them, the training batches contain exactly 5000 images from each class.The classes are completely mutually exclusive. There is no overlap between automobiles and trucks. "Automobile" includes sedans, SUVs, etc. and "Truck" includes only big trucks. Neither includes pickup trucks.

The CIFAR-10 dataset looks like Figure 4-3.

Figure 4-3. The classes in the CIFAR-10 dataset and a few examples of each. The CIFAR-10 dataset is one of the popular datasets which is used to test the efficacy of a Neural Network

The CIFAR-100 dataset is just like the CIFAR-10, except it has 100 classes containing 600 images each. There are 500 training images and 100 testing images per class. The 100 classes in the CIFAR-100 are grouped into 20 superclasses. Each image comes with a "fine" label (the class to which it belongs) and a "coarse" label (the superclass to which it belongs).

Figure 4-4 provides a list of classes in the CIFAR-100. Each of the superclasses has subclasses. For example, apples, mushrooms, oranges, pears, and so on are the subclasses, and their superclass is fruit and vegetable.

Superclass	Classes
aquatic mammals	beaver, dolphin, otter, seal, whale
fish	aquarium fish, flatfish, ray, shark, trout
flowers	orchids, poppies, roses, sunflowers, tulips
food containers	bottles, bowls, cans, cups, plates
fruit and vegetables	apples, mushrooms, oranges, pears, sweet peppers
household electrical devices	clock, computer keyboard, lamp, telephone, television
household furniture	bed, chair, couch, table, wardrobe
insects	bee, beetle, butterfly, caterpillar, cockroach
large carnivores	bear, leopard, lion, tiger, wolf
large man-made outdoor things	bridge, castle, house, road, skyscraper
large natural outdoor scenes	cloud, forest, mountain, plain, sea
large omnivores and herbivores	camel, cattle, chimpanzee, elephant, kangaroo
medium-sized mammals	fox, porcupine, possum, raccoon, skunk
non-insect invertebrates	crab, lobster, snail, spider, worm
people	baby, boy, girl, man, woman
reptiles	crocodile, dinosaur, lizard, snake, turtle
small mammals	hamster, mouse, rabbit, shrew, squirrel
trees	maple, oak, palm, pine, willow
vehicles 1	bicycle, bus, motorcycle, pickup truck, train
vehicles 2	lawn-mower, rocket, streetcar, tank, tractor

Figure 4-4. *The list of all the superclass and classes in the CIFAR-100 dataset*

It is time for developing use cases by using AlexNet and VGG16.

4.8 Working on CIFAR-10 using AlexNet

Let's develop a classification solution on CIFAR-10 using AlexNet.

1. Import all the necessary libraries here and load the CIFAR-10 dataset.

```
import keras
from keras.datasets import cifar10
from keras import backend as K
from keras.layers import Input,
Conv2D, GlobalAveragePooling2D, Dense,
BatchNormalization, Activation, MaxPooling2D
from keras.models import Model
from keras.layers import
concatenate,Dropout,Flatten
```

2. Here, we import ModelCheckpoint which will be used to create checkpoints to save the best model based on the validation accuracy. We are studying the checkpoint in detail once we configure the settings.

```
from keras import optimizers,regularizers
from keras.preprocessing.image import
ImageDataGenerator
from keras.initializers import he_normal
from keras.callbacks import
LearningRateScheduler, TensorBoard,
ModelCheckpoint
```

3. Next, we load the CIFAR-10 data with the cifar.load_data() step.

```
(x_train, y_train), (x_test, y_test) =
cifar10.load_data()
```

4. Now, preprocess the images by getting the mean and standard deviation and then standardizing them.

```
mean = np.mean(x_train,axis=(0,1,2,3))
std = np.std(x_train, axis=(0, 1, 2, 3))
x_train = (x_train-mean)/(std+1e-7)
x_test = (x_test-mean)/(std+1e-7)
```

> **Note**   Experiment executing the code with and without step 4 to examine the difference in performance between processed and unprocessed images.

5. Now, let's create our training and testing target variable data. This step is similar to the solutions we have developed in the previous chapter.

```
y_train = keras.utils.to_categorical(y_train,
num_classes)
y_test = keras.utils.to_categorical(y_test,
num_classes)
```

Let us have a look at the dataset.

```
fig = plt.figure(figsize=(18, 8))
columns = 5
rows = 5
for i in range(1, columns*rows + 1):
    fig.add_subplot(rows, columns, i)
    plt.imshow(X_train[i], interpolation='lanczos')
```

Figure 4-5 shows some of the images from our dataset. Look at the different classes of images we have. Also, examine the resolution and aspect ratio of the images.

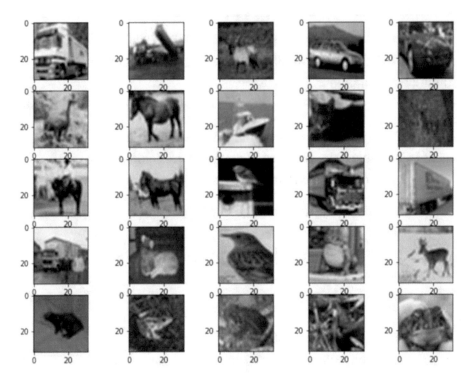

Figure 4-5. *A few example images from the dataset are shown here*

6. Now let us create the AlexNet architecture. Here, we
    will try a different method. We will define a function
    to create the network. While creating the AlexNet,
    we start with the convolutional layer with the
    parameters defined in the network. The first layer
    has a kernel size of 11x11, 96 channels, and a stride
    of 4x4. And the network follows.

```python
def alexnet(img_input,classes=10):
    xnet = Conv2D(96,(11,11),strides=(4,4),padding='same',
            activation='relu',kernel_initializer='uniform')
            (img_input)
    xnet = MaxPooling2D(pool_size=(3,3),strides=(2,2),
            padding='same',data_format=DATA_ FORMAT)(xnet)

    xnet = Conv2D(256,(5,5),strides=(1,1),padding='same',
            activation='relu',kernel_initializer='uniform')
            (xnet)
    xnet = MaxPooling2D(pool_size=(3,3),strides=(2,2),
            padding='same',data_format=DATA_ FORMAT)(xnet)

    xnet = Conv2D(384,(3,3),strides=(1,1),padding='same',
            activation='relu',kernel_initializer='uniform')
            (xnet)

    xnet = Conv2D(384,(3,3),strides=(1,1),padding='same',
            activation='relu',kernel_initializer='uniform')
            (xnet)

    xnet = Conv2D(256,(3,3),strides=(1,1),padding='same',
            activation='relu',kernel_initializer='uniform')
            (xnet)
    xnet = MaxPooling2D(pool_size=(3,3),strides=(2,2),
            padding='same',data_format=DATA_ FORMAT)(xnet)
    xnet = Flatten()(xnet)
    xnet = Dense(4096,activation='relu')(xnet)
    xnet = Dropout(0.25)(xnet)
    xnet = Dense(4096,activation='relu')(xnet)
    xnet = Dropout(0.25)(xnet)
    out_model = Dense(classes, activation='softmax')(xnet)
    return out_model
```

The output of the preceding function will be the network.

7. Now let's input the image in a 32x32x3 shape. Then, use the AlexNet function to get the desired model.

```
img_input=Input(shape=(32,32,3))
output = alexnet(img_input)
model=Model(img_input,output)
```

8. We then generate a summary of the model.

```
model.summary()
```

Here's the summary. We have all the layers, respective output shape, and the number of parameters (Figure 4-6).

Model: "model_7"

Layer (type)	Output Shape	Param #
input_7 (InputLayer)	(None, 32, 32, 3)	0
conv2d_50 (Conv2D)	(None, 8, 8, 96)	34944
max_pooling2d_28 (MaxPooling	(None, 4, 4, 96)	0
conv2d_51 (Conv2D)	(None, 4, 4, 256)	614656
max_pooling2d_29 (MaxPooling	(None, 2, 2, 256)	0
conv2d_52 (Conv2D)	(None, 2, 2, 384)	885120
conv2d_53 (Conv2D)	(None, 2, 2, 384)	1327488
conv2d_54 (Conv2D)	(None, 2, 2, 256)	884992
max_pooling2d_30 (MaxPooling	(None, 1, 1, 256)	0
flatten_9 (Flatten)	(None, 256)	0
dense_22 (Dense)	(None, 4096)	1052672
dropout_24 (Dropout)	(None, 4096)	0
dense_23 (Dense)	(None, 4096)	16781312
dropout_25 (Dropout)	(None, 4096)	0
dense_24 (Dense)	(None, 10)	40970

Total params: 21,622,154
Trainable params: 21,622,154
Non-trainable params: 0

Figure 4-6. *The summary of the AlexNet model. It has 21 million parameters to train*

The model summary denotes that we have 21 million parameters to train this AlexNet model.

9. We need to compile the model now, and the
    optimizer is one of the arguments used to compile
    Keras-based models. We are using Stochastic
    Gradient Descent (SGD) here with a learning rate of
    0.01 and a momentum of 0.8. Feel free to iterate with
    different values of learning rate and momentum.
    SGD includes support for momentum, learning rate
    decay, and Nesterov momentum. You must be aware
    of what learning rate is as we have discussed it in
    the previous chapters. Momentum is the parameter
    that accelerates SGD in the relevant direction and
    dampens oscillations. The last parameter, Nesterov,
    denotes whether to apply Nesterov momentum.

```
sgd = optimizers.SGD(lr=.01, momentum=0.8,
nesterov=True) model.compile(loss='categorical_
crossentropy', optimizer=sgd,
metrics=['accuracy'])
```

Note   We have used SGD over here. Experiment with Adam,
RMSProp, Adagrad, and Adadelta to compare the training time and
respective performance.

---

10. Next, we set the checkpoint. We do this so that only
    when the validation accuracy increases, the last
    saved model is replaced.

    Wondering what is checkpoint?

    While we develop our model, the validation
    accuracy decreases often in the next epoch, and
    hence we would like to use the accuracy in the

earlier epoch. For example, if in the fifth epoch we get 74% accuracy which decreases to 73% in the sixth epoch, we would like to use the fifth epoch and not the sixth. Using checkpoint, we can save the model only when the accuracy has increased and not with each subsequent epoch. If we do not have a checkpoint, we will get only the final model in the final epoch. And it might not be the best performing model. Hence, it is advised to use checkpoints.

```
filepath="weights.best.hdf5"
checkpoint = ModelCheckpoint(filepath,
monitor='val_acc', verbose=1, save_best_
only=True, mode='max')
callbacks_list = [checkpoint]
epochs = 50
```

11. Now, let's use ImageDataGenerator for data augmentation. It generates batches of tensor image data with real-time data augmentation. The data will be looped over (in batches).

```
datagen = ImageDataGenerator(horizontal_
flip=True, width_shift_range=0.115,
height_shift_range=0.115, fill_
mode='constant',cval=0.)
datagen.fit(x_train)
```

12. Start training the network. Note that we have set callbacks as callbacks_list which we described for the model checkpoint.

```
model.fit_generator(datagen.flow(x_train,
 y_train,batch_size=batch_size), steps_per_
epoch=iterations,
```

```
    epochs=epochs,
    callbacks=callbacks_list,
    validation_data=(x_test, y_test))
```

You will get the following output after training the network. For brevity, we have only shown the final epochs.

```
Epoch 00046: val_acc did not improve from 0.74870
Epoch 47/50
782/782 [==============================] - 23s 29ms/step - loss: 0.3578 - acc: 0.8708 - val_loss: 0.9420 - val_acc:
0.7369

Epoch 00047: val_acc did not improve from 0.74870
Epoch 48/50
782/782 [==============================] - 23s 30ms/step - loss: 0.3505 - acc: 0.8725 - val_loss: 0.9153 - val_acc:
0.7464

Epoch 00048: val_acc did not improve from 0.74870
Epoch 49/50
782/782 [==============================] - 23s 30ms/step - loss: 0.3436 - acc: 0.8757 - val_loss: 0.9361 - val_acc:
0.7390

Epoch 00049: val_acc did not improve from 0.74870
Epoch 50/50
782/782 [==============================] - 23s 30ms/step - loss: 0.3331 - acc: 0.8796 - val_loss: 0.9685 - val_acc:
0.7429
```

Note that we get validation accuracy of 74.29% after 50 epochs. Also note that if the accuracy is not improving, the model is not changing the best accuracy which is 74.80%.

13. Let us now measure our performance. First, we measure our accuracy; it will be followed by the loss. The code and graphs are similar to the ones generated in the previous chapter.

```
import matplotlib.pyplot as plt
f, ax = plt.subplots()
ax.plot([None] + model.history.history['acc'], 'o-')
ax.plot([None] + model.history.history['val_acc'], 'x-')
ax.legend(['Train acc', 'Validation acc'], loc = 0)
ax.set_title('Training/Validation acc per Epoch')
ax.set_xlabel('Epoch')
ax.set_ylabel('acc')
```

Here's the output (Figure 4-7).

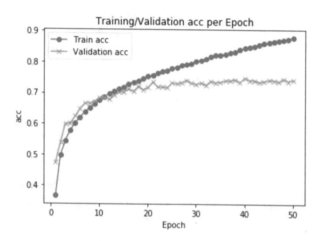

Figure 4-7. *We are plotting the accuracy of the training dataset vs. the validation dataset*

14.   Now, let's measure the loss.

```
import matplotlib.pyplot as plt
f, ax = plt.subplots()
ax.plot([None] + model.history.history['loss'], 'o-')
ax.plot([None] + model.history.history['val_loss'], 'x-')
ax.legend(['Train loss', 'Validation loss'], loc = 0)
ax.set_title('Training/Validation loss per Epoch')
ax.set_xlabel('Epoch')
ax.set_ylabel('acc')
```

Here's the output (Figure 4-8).

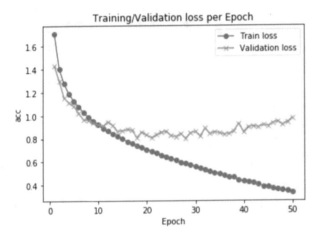

Figure 4-8. *The training and validation loss are shown here*

15. We will now use this model to make the predictions
    and generate the confusion matrix for our
    predictions using the predict function.

```
predictions = model.predict(x_test)
```

16. When you try to generate the confusion matrix
    using the following function, the following error is
    received:

```
from sklearn.metrics import confusion_matrix
import numpy as np
confusion_matrix(y_test,
np.argmax(predictions,axis=1))
```

```
ValueError                              Traceback (most recent call last)
<ipython-input-79-cb748a72dafc> in <module>()
----> 1 confusion_matrix(y_test, np.argmax(predictions,axis=1))

/usr/local/lib/python3.6/dist-packages/sklearn/metrics/classification.py in confusion_matrix(y_true, y_pred, labels,
sample_weight)
    251
    252     """
--> 253     y_type, y_true, y_pred = _check_targets(y_true, y_pred)
    254     if y_type not in ("binary", "multiclass"):
    255         raise ValueError("%s is not supported" % y_type)

/usr/local/lib/python3.6/dist-packages/sklearn/metrics/classification.py in _check_targets(y_true, y_pred)
     79     if len(y_type) > 1:
     80         raise ValueError("Classification metrics can't handle a mix of {0} "
---> 81                          "and {1} targets".format(type_true, type_pred))
     82
     83     # We can't have more than one value on y_type => The set is no more needed

ValueError: Classification metrics can't handle a mix of multilabel-indicator and multiclass targets
```

We get this error because the Confusion Matrix
requires both the predicted values and the image
labels as single digits and not as one-hot encoded
vectors. Our test_values have to be converted here,
and it should resolve the error for us.

Note   Print values of predictions and y_test[1] to examine the
difference.

---

17. Let's convert the labels to the single digit 1, and then
    we will generate the confusion matrix.

    ```
    rounded_labels=np.argmax(y_test, axis=1)
    rounded_labels[1]
    cm = confusion_matrix(rounded_labels,
    np.argmax(predictions,axis=1))
    cm
    ```

    You will get the following Confusion Matrix as
    the output of the last statement. Being a ten-class
    problem, it will generate the values for all the
    respective ten classes.

```
array([[843,   19,   21,    8,   14,    5,   10,   11,   48,   21],
       [ 19,  878,    2,    3,    3,    5,    6,    4,   21,   59],
       [ 79,   11,  618,   41,   77,   43,   67,   36,   15,   13],
       [ 29,   29,   62,  499,   54,  168,   73,   42,   17,   27],
       [ 23,    6,   61,   47,  686,   34,   43,   82,   15,    3],
       [ 14,   14,   29,  127,   50,  632,   45,   65,   10,   14],
       [  8,   10,   47,   41,   33,   23,  815,    7,    5,   11],
       [ 17,    5,   14,   24,   35,   60,    9,  817,    7,   12],
       [ 53,   45,    6,    9,    2,    3,    2,    2,  860,   18],
       [ 38,  117,    4,    6,    3,    4,    7,    6,   34,  781]]])
```

18. Now define the confusion matrix function and
     generate the confusion matrix:

```
def plot_confusion_matrix(cm):
    cm = [row/sum(row) for row in cm]
    fig = plt.figure(figsize=(10, 10))
    ax = fig.add_subplot(111)
    cax = ax.matshow(cm, cmap=plt.cm.Oranges)
    fig.colorbar(cax)
    plt.title('Confusion Matrix')
    plt.xlabel('Predicted Class IDs')
    plt.ylabel('True Class IDs')
    plt.show()

plot_confusion_matrix(cm)
```

The output of the preceding code is shown in Figure 4-9.

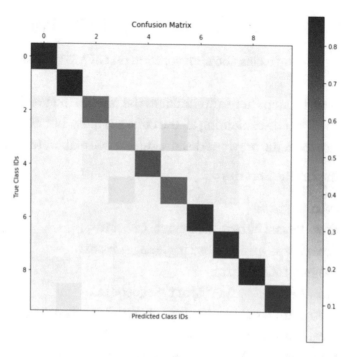

Figure 4-9. *The confusion matrix for the problem is shown here. The network is making good predictions for some of the classes. It is advised that the network is tested by tuning the hyperparameters*

From the Confusion Matrix, it is clear that the network is making correct predictions for some of the classes. You are advised to tune the hyperparameters and examine which classes get impacted as a result of the changed network.

In this use case, we used AlexNet to work on the CIFAR-10 dataset, and we got 74.80% validation accuracy. Let's train our VGG network next and measure its performance.

4.9 **Working on CIFAR-10 using VGG**

We will now develop a classification solution on CIFAR-10 using the VGG network.

As most of the steps here are similar to the ones in the previous section, we will not be explaining all the code snippets, but wherever there is a difference from the previous discussion, we will elaborate on them.

1. Import the libraries.

```
import keras
from keras.datasets import cifar10
from keras.preprocessing.image import
ImageDataGenerator
from keras.models import Sequential
from keras.callbacks import ModelCheckpoint
from keras.layers import Dense, Dropout,
Activation, Flatten from keras.layers import
Conv2D, MaxPooling2D, BatchNormalization
from keras import optimizers
import numpy as np
from keras.layers.core import Lambda
from keras import backend as K
from keras import regularizers
import matplotlib.pyplot as plt
import warnings warnings.
filterwarnings("ignore")
```

2. Set your hyperparameters.

```
number_classes = 10
wght_decay = 0.00005
x_shape = [32,32,3]
batch_size = 64
```

```
maxepoches = 30
learning_rate = 0.1
learning_decay = 1e-6
learning_drop = 20
```

3. Load the data and generate a few images.

```
(x_train, y_train), (x_test, y_test) = cifar10.
load_data()
x_train = x_train.astype('float32')
x_test = x_test.astype('float32')
fig = plt.figure(figsize=(18, 8))
columns = 5
rows = 5
for i in range(1, columns*rows + 1):
    fig.add_subplot(rows, columns, i)
    plt.imshow(x_train[i],
interpolation='lanczos')
```

4. Standardize the image data.

```
mean = np.mean(x_train,axis=(0,1,2,3))
std = np.std(x_train, axis=(0, 1, 2, 3))
x_train = (x_train-mean)/(std+1e-7)
x_test = (x_test-mean)/(std+1e-7)
y_train = keras.utils.to_categorical(y_train,
number_classes)
y_test = keras.utils.to_categorical(y_test,
number_classes)
```

5. Create your VGG16 model now.

```
model = Sequential()
model.add(Conv2D(64, (3, 3), padding='same',
```

```
input_shape=x_shape,kernel_
regularizer=regularizers.l2(wght_decay)))
model.add(Activation('relu'))
model.add(BatchNormalization())
model.add(Dropout(0.3))
model.add(Conv2D(64, (3, 3),
padding='same',kernel_regularizer=regularizers.
l2(wght_decay)))
model.add(Activation('relu'))
model.add(BatchNormalization())
model.add(MaxPooling2D(pool_size=(2, 2)))
model.add(Conv2D(128, (3, 3),
padding='same',kernel_regularizer=regularizers.
l2(wght_decay)))
model.add(Activation('relu'))
model.add(BatchNormalization())
model.add(Dropout(0.4))
model.add(Conv2D(128, (3, 3),
padding='same',kernel_regularizer=regularizers.
l2(wght_decay)))
model.add(Activation('relu'))
model.add(BatchNormalization())
model.add(MaxPooling2D(pool_size=(2, 2)))
model.add(Conv2D(256, (3, 3),
padding='same',kernel_regularizer=regularizers.
l2(wght_decay))) model.add(Activation('relu'))
model.add(BatchNormalization())
model.add(Dropout(0.4))
model.add(Conv2D(256, (3, 3),
padding='same',kernel_regularizer=regularizers.
l2(wght_decay))) model.add(Activation('relu'))
```

```
model.add(BatchNormalization())
model.add(Dropout(0.4))
model.add(Conv2D(256, (3, 3),
padding='same',kernel_regularizer=regularizers.
l2(wght_decay))) model.add(Activation('relu'))
model.add(BatchNormalization())
model.add(MaxPooling2D(pool_size=(2, 2)))
model.add(Conv2D(512, (3, 3),
padding='same',kernel_regularizer=regularizers.
l2(wght_decay))) model.add(Activation('relu'))
model.add(BatchNormalization())
model.add(Dropout(0.4))
model.add(Conv2D(512, (3, 3),
padding='same',kernel_regularizer=regularizers.
l2(wght_decay))) model.add(Activation('relu'))
model.add(BatchNormalization())
model.add(Dropout(0.4))
model.add(Conv2D(512, (3, 3),
padding='same',kernel_regularizer=regularizers.
l2(wght_decay))) model.add(Activation('relu'))
model.add(BatchNormalization())
model.add(MaxPooling2D(pool_size=(2, 2)))
model.add(Conv2D(512, (3, 3),
padding='same',kernel_regularizer=regularizers.
l2(wght_decay)))
model.add(Activation('relu'))
model.add(BatchNormalization())
model.add(Dropout(0.4))
model.add(Conv2D(512, (3, 3),
padding='same',kernel_regularizer=regularizers.
l2(wght_decay)))
```

```
model.add(Activation('relu'))
model.add(BatchNormalization())
model.add(Dropout(0.4))
model.add(Conv2D(512, (3, 3),
padding='same',kernel_regularizer=regularizers.
l2(wght_decay))) model.add(Activation('relu'))
model.add(BatchNormalization())
model.add(MaxPooling2D(pool_size=(2, 2)))
model.add(Dropout(0.5))
model.add(Flatten()) model.
add(Dense(512,kernel_regularizer=regularizers.
l2(wght_decay))) model.add(Activation('relu'))
model.add(BatchNormalization())
model.add(Dropout(0.5)) model.add(Dense(number_
classes)) model.add(Activation('softmax'))
```

6. Generate the model summary.

```
model.summary()
```

7. From the image augmentation step to fitting the
    VGG network, the steps are exactly the same as in
    the AlexNet example in the previous section.

```
image_augm = ImageDataGenerator( featurewise_
center=False, samplewise_center=False,
featurewise_std_normalization=False,
samplewise_std_normalization=False, zca_
whitening=False, rotation_range=12, width_
shift_range=0.2, height_shift_range=0.1,
horizontal_flip=True, vertical_flip=False)
image_augm.fit(x_train)
```

```
sgd = optimizers.SGD(lr=learning_rate,
decay=learning_decay, momentum=0.9,
nesterov=True)
model.compile(loss='categorical_crossentropy',
optimizer=sgd,metrics=['accuracy'])
filepath="weights.best.hdf5"
checkpoint = ModelCheckpoint(filepath,
monitor='val_acc', verbose=1,
save_best_only=True, mode='max')
callbacks_list = [checkpoint]
trained_model = model.fit_generator(image_augm.
flow(x_train, y_train, batch_size=batch_size),
steps_per_epoch=x_train.shape[0]//batch_size,
epochs=maxepoches,
validation_data=(x_test, y_
test),callbacks=callbacks_list,verbose=1)
```

You will get this output when you train your model.
We are showing the final epochs only.

```
Epoch 27/30
781/781 [==============================] - 36s 46ms/step - loss: 1.1554 - acc: 0.7690 - val_loss: 0.9821 - val_acc:
0.8274

Epoch 00027: val_acc improved from 0.80260 to 0.82740, saving model to weights.best.hdf5
Epoch 28/30
781/781 [==============================] - 36s 46ms/step - loss: 1.1403 - acc: 0.7699 - val_loss: 1.1028 - val_acc:
0.7885

Epoch 00028: val_acc did not improve from 0.82740
Epoch 29/30
781/781 [==============================] - 36s 46ms/step - loss: 1.1073 - acc: 0.7805 - val_loss: 1.0811 - val_acc:
0.7917

Epoch 00029: val_acc did not improve from 0.82740
Epoch 30/30
781/781 [==============================] - 36s 46ms/step - loss: 1.0992 - acc: 0.7835 - val_loss: 0.9948 - val_acc:
0.8231

Epoch 00030: val_acc did not improve from 0.82740
```

The best validation accuracy is 82.74%.

8. Plot the accuracy measures and finally the
    confusion matrix. The code is exactly the same as
    the one used for AlexNet.

Here's the accuracy plot (Figure 4-10).

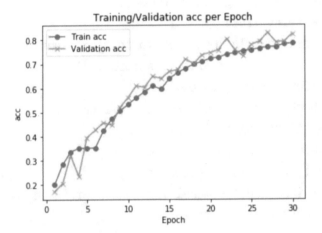

Figure 4-10. *The training and validation accuracy plot for the VGG network*

Here's the loss plot (Figure 4-11).

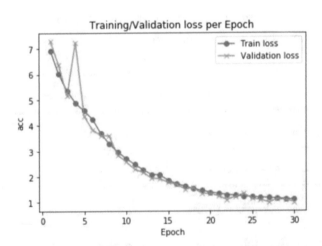

Figure 4-11. *The training and validation loss plot for the VGG network*

Here's the Confusion Matrix:

```
array([[796,   20,   30,    5,   19,    0,   10,   16,   60,   44],
       [  1,  932,    0,    0,    1,    1,    1,    1,   19,   44],
       [ 42,    4,  724,   18,   53,    9,  108,   25,   10,    7],
       [ 25,    7,   37,  612,   49,   63,  112,   50,   23,   22],
       [  4,    1,   25,   13,  818,    7,   73,   54,    3,    2],
       [  6,   12,   39,  134,   47,  632,   48,   71,    2,    9],
       [  4,    2,   13,   16,   11,    2,  943,    5,    2,    2],
       [  4,    1,    8,   11,   19,    7,    9,  935,    2,    4],
       [ 34,   10,    4,    0,    5,    0,    5,    5,  898,   39],
       [  5,   31,    0,    1,    3,    0,    4,    6,    9,  941]])
```

Here's the confusion matrix plot (Figure 4-12).

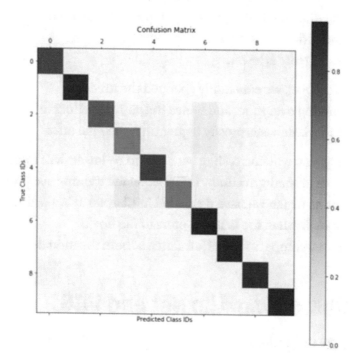

Figure 4-12. *Confusion matrix generated for the VGG plot*

Note that the validation loss is **lesser** than the training accuracy. We would normally expect training accuracy to be higher than testing accuracy, but here we are witnessing the opposite case. The reasons for it are as follows:

1. When we use Keras to generate Deep Learning solutions, there are two modes, namely, training and testing. During the testing phase, dropout or L1/L2 weight regularizations are turned off.

2. We calculate the average loss over each batch of training data to get the training loss, whereas to calculate the testing loss, it is done using the model and is done at the end of the epoch; hence, the testing loss is lower.

3. Moreover, we constantly changed the model by training over time, and hence the computed loss in initial batches is mostly higher than the final ones.

Generally, you will find testing accuracy to be lower than training accuracy. In case testing accuracy is far below the training accuracy, we call it *overfitting* which we have discussed in Chapter 1. We will again visit this concept in detail in the later chapters of the book.

We will now compare the performance of both the models.

4.10 Comparing AlexNet and VGG

If we compare the performance of AlexNet and VGGNet, we will find that

1. The validation accuracy of VGG is higher than AlexNet (82.74% vs. 74.80%).

2. The Confusion Matrix shows that VGG has predicted a higher number of correct classes as compared to AlexNet.

But it does not mean that we can generalize VGG's performance to be always better than AlexNet. Depending on the dataset and the business problem at hand, we test both the networks.

Note that for the examples we discussed, AlexNet was trained for 50 epochs as compared to 30 epochs for VGGNet. Try to train for the same number of epochs and analyze the difference.

While taking a decision to pick and choose a network, we compare and contrast the two architectures. We compare the training time required, the dataset requirement, the epoch-wise movement, and finally the accuracy KPIs. And then we reach a conclusion.

Both the architectures are often cited and revered in the Deep Learning community.

4.11 Working with CIFAR-100

You are advised to use a similar code for the CIFAR-100 dataset. There are a few changes in the code that are as follows.

While importing the libraries, instead of importing cifar10, import cifar100.

```
from keras.datasets import cifar100
```

Similarly, load the dataset for CIFAR-100.

```
(x_train, y_train), (x_test, y_test) = cifar100.load_data()
```

The number of classes is 100 and not 10. Wherever the number of classes is mentioned, change it to 100. Then fit the model and analyze the results.

With this, we have completed the implementations of Python code using the datasets. We can now proceed to the summary of the chapter.

4.12 Summary

In this chapter, we introduced AlexNet and VGGNet and created solutions using the CIFAR datasets.

The two networks are often used to benchmark any computer vision–based solution. They are simple to understand and quick to implement.

AlexNet and VGG have been cited many times across papers and literature. They are widely used in many practical solutions too. During practical implementation, the quality of the dataset will define the prediction power of the network. Hence, if you are using the networks for implementation on a custom dataset, due diligence is required in the collection of the images.

An important point to note is that the dataset should be representative of the real-world business scenarios. If the dataset does not capture the real-world business scenarios, the solution will not be able to solve the business problem. And a lot of time and resources are spent on getting the dataset. We are going to visit these concepts again in the last chapter of the book – where the requirements are dealt in detail.

Now, let us move to the next architectures and develop more practical use cases. Let's continue this journey!

You should be able to answer the questions in the exercise now!

REVIEW EXERCISES

1. What is the difference between AlexNet and VGG16?

2. Explain the significance of a checkpoint.

3. Use the German traffic sign dataset used in the last chapter and fit VGG16 and VGG19 to it. Compare the accuracies of the two models.

4. Find out the industry implementations of VGG16 and AlexNet.

5. Download the multiclass weather dataset for image
    classification from `https://data.mendeley.com/`
    `datasets/4drtyfjtfy/1`. Develop AlexNet and VGG
    networks and compare the accuracies.

6. Get the concrete crack image dataset for classification from
    `https://data.mendeley.com/datasets/5y9wdsg2zt/2`
    and develop the VGG16 and VGG19 solution.

4.12.1 Further readings

1. AlexNet original paper is at `https://papers.nips.`
    `cc/paper/4824-imagenet- classification-with-`
    `deep-convolutional-neural-networks.pdf`.

2. VGG16 original paper is at `https://arxiv.org/`
    `pdf/1409.1556.pdf`.

3. Papers dealing with CIFAR-10 can be accessed
    at `https://paperswithcode.com/sota/image-`
    `classification-on-cifar-10`.

4. Papers dealing with CIFAR-100 can be accessed
    at `https://paperswithcode.com/sota/image-`
    `classification-on-cifar-100`.

CHAPTER 5

Object Detection Using Deep Learning

Just because something doesn't do what you planned it to do doesn't mean it's useless.

—Thomas Edison

To solve a particular problem, we try multiple solutions, and many times after a few iterations, we find the best solution. Machine learning and Deep Learning are no different. During the discovery phase, improvements and constant modifications are done to improve the performance of the previous version of the algorithms. The weakness observed in the last phase, the slowness in the computation, the incorrect classifications made – all pave the way for a better solution.

In the last two chapters, we understood and created solutions to classify images into binary or multiple classes. But most of the images had only one object in them. And we did not identify the location of an object in the image. We simply said whether or not the object is present in that image.

In this chapter, we will be identifying an object in any image. At the same time, its position will also be determined by creating a bounding box around it. It is a step ahead from the image classification solutions we have developed so far.

© Vaibhav Verdhan 2021
V. Verdhan, *Computer Vision Using Deep Learning*,
https://doi.org/10.1007/978-1-4842-6616-8_5

There are quite a few architectures for Object Detection like R-CNN, Fast R-CNN, Faster R-CNN, SSD (Single Shot MultiBox Detector), and YOLO (You Only Look Once).

We are going to study these network architectures in this chapter and create Python solutions for the same.

We will cover the following topics in this chapter:

1. Object Detection and the use cases

2. R-CNN, Fast R-CNN, and Faster R-CNN
    architectures

3. Single Shot MultiBox Detector

4. You Only Look Once (YOLO)

5. Python implementation of the algorithms

Welcome to the fifth chapter and all the very best!

5.1 Technical requirements

The code and datasets for the chapter are uploaded at the GitHub link `https://github.com/Apress/computer-vision-using-deep-learning/tree/main/Chapter5` for this book. As always, we will be using the Python Jupyter Notebook for this chapter. For this chapter, a GPU might be required to execute the code, and you can use Google Colaboratory. The instructions to set Google Colab. Same as last chapter of the book.

Let's proceed with the Deep Learning architectures in the next section.

5.2 Object Detection

Object Detection is one of the most cited and acknowledged solutions in the area of Machine Learning and Deep Learning. It is quite a novel solution and very interesting to solve. The use cases for object detection are quite a few. And hence, organizations and researchers are spending huge time and resources to uncover this capability. As the name suggests, Object Detection is a computer vision technique to locate objects in an image or in a video. The detection can be intended to be done in a live stream video too. When we humans look at a picture, we can quickly identify the objects and their respective position in an image. We can quickly categorize if it is an apple or a car or a human being. We can also determine from any angle. The reason is that our minds have been trained in such a way that it can identify various objects. Even if the size of an object gets smaller or bigger, we are able to locate them and detect them.

The goal is to replicate this decision-making intelligence using Machine Learning and Deep Learning. We will be examining the concepts of object detection, localization, and classification and developing Python codes.

But before examining the basics of object detection, we should first study the difference between object classification, object localization, and object detection. They are the building concepts for object detection. We are studying the difference in the three components in the next section now.

5.2.1 Object classification vs. object localization vs. object detection

Look at the images in Figure 5-1 of a vacuum cleaner. In the previous chapters, we have developed the image classification solutions to classify such images into "a Vacuum Cleaner" or "not." So we could have easily labeled the first image as a vacuum cleaner.

On the other hand, localization refers to finding the position of the object in an image. So when we do Image Localization, it means that the algorithm is having a dual responsibility of classifying an image as well as drawing a bounding box around it, which is depicted in the second image. In the first image of Figure 5-1, we have a vacuum cleaner, and in the second image, we have localized it.

Figure 5-1. *Object detection means identifying and localization of the object. In the first image, we can classify if it is a vacuum cleaner, while in the second image, we are drawing a box around it, which is the localization of the image*

To scale the solution, we can have multiple objects in the same image and even multiple objects of different categories in the same image, and we have to identify all of them. And draw the bounding boxes around them. An example can be of a solution trained to detect cars. On a busy road, there will be many cars, and hence the solution should be able to detect each of them and draw bounding boxes around them.

Object detection is surely a fantastic solution. We will now discuss the major object detection use cases in the next section.

5.2.2 Use cases of Object Detection

Deep Learning has expanded many capabilities across domains and organizations. Object detection is a key one and is a very powerful solution which is making huge ripples in our business and personal world. The major use cases of object detection are

1. Object Detection is the key intelligence behind autonomous driving technology. It allows the users to detect the cars, pedestrians, the background, motorbikes, and so on to improve road safety.

2. We can detect objects in the hands of people, and the solution can be used for security and monitoring purposes. Surveillance systems can be made much more intelligent and accurate. Crowd control systems can be made more sophisticated, and the reaction time will be reduced.

3. A solution might be used for detecting objects in a shopping basket, and it can be used by the retailers for the automated transactions. This will speed up the overall process with less manual intervention.

4. Object Detection is also used in testing of mechanical systems and on manufacturing lines. We can detect objects present on the products which might be contaminating the product quality.

5. In the medical world, the identification of diseases by analyzing the images of a body part will help in faster treatment of the diseases.

There are very less areas where the usage is not envisioned. It is one of the areas which are highly researched, and every day new progress is being made in this domain. Organizations and researchers across the globe are making huge ripples in this area and creating path-breaking solutions.

We have examined the major use cases of object detection. Now let's look at some methods for object detection.

5.3 Object Detection methods

We can perform object detection using both Machine Learning and Deep Learning. We will be discussing the Deep Learning methods in this book, but for curious readers, here are a few solutions:

1. Image segmentation using simple attributes like shape, size, and color of an object.

2. We can use an aggregated channel feature (ACF), which is a variation of channel features. ACF does not calculate the rectangular sums at various locations or scales. Instead, it extracts features directly as pixel values.

3. Viola-Jones algorithm can be used for face detection. The suggested papers are at the end of the chapter.

There are other solutions like RANSAC (random sample consensus), Haar feature–based cascade classifier, SVM classification using HOG features, and so on which can be used for object detection. In this book, we are focusing on Deep Learning methods.

The following Deep Learning architectures are commonly being used for Object Detection:

1. R-CNN: Regions with CNN features. It combines Regional Proposals with CNN.

2. Fast R-CNN: A Fast Region–based Convolutional Neural Network.

3. Faster R-CNN: Object detection networks on Region Proposal algorithms to hypothesize object locations.

4. Mask R-CNN: This network extends Faster R-CNN by adding the prediction of segmentation masks on each region of interest.

5. YOLO: You Only Look Once architecture. It proposes a single Neural Network to predict bounding boxes and class probabilities from an image in a single evaluation.

6. SSD: Single Shot MultiBox Detector. It presents a model to predict objects in images using a single deep Neural Network.

Now, we will examine the Deep Learning frameworks in the next section. There are some base concepts to be studied which form the base of object detection techniques. We will study them too. Post the discussion of Deep Learning frameworks, we will create Python solutions.

5.4 Deep Learning frameworks for Object Detection

We will now start with Deep Learning–based object detection algorithms and architectures. They are made of a few components and concepts. Before diving deep into the architectures, let us first recognize a few of the important components of Object Detection. The key ones are

- Sliding window approach for Object Detection

- Bounding box approach

- Intersection over Union (IoU)

- Non-max suppression

- Anchor boxes concept

We will start with the sliding window approach in the next section.

5.4.1 Sliding window approach for Object Detection

When we want to detect objects, a very simple approach can be: why not divide the image into regions or specific areas and then classify each one of them. This approach for object detection is *sliding window*. As the name suggests, it is a rectangular box which slides through the entire image. The box is of fixed length and width with a stride to move over the entire image.

Look at the image of the vacuum cleaner in Figure 5-2. We are using a sliding window at each part of the image. The red box is sliding over the entire image of the vacuum cleaner. From left to right and then vertically, we can observe that different parts of the image are becoming the point of observation. Since the window is sliding, it is referred to as the sliding window approach.

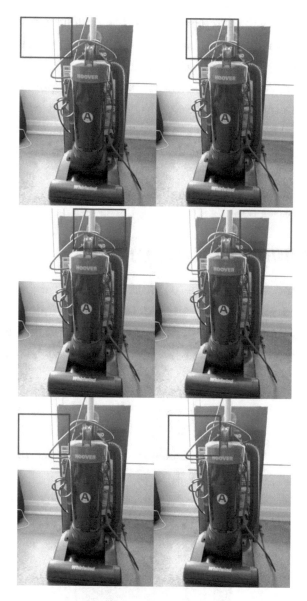

Figure 5-2. *The sliding window approach to detect an object and identify it. Notice how the sliding box is moving across the entire image; the process is able to detect but is really a time-consuming process and computationally expensive too*

Then for each of these regions cropped, we can classify whether this region contains an object that interests us or not. And then we increase the size of the sliding window and continue the process.

Sliding window has proven to work, but it is a computationally very expensive technique and will be slow to implement as we are classifying all the regions in an image. Also, to localize the objects, we need a small window size and small stride. But still it is a simple approach to understand.

The next approach is the bounding box approach.

5.5 Bounding box approach

We discussed the sliding window approach. It outputs less accurate bounding boxes as it is dependent on the size of the window. And hence we have another approach wherein we divide the entire image into grids (x by x), and then for each grid, we define our target label. We can show a bounding box in Figure 5-3.

Figure 5-3. *Bounding box can generate the x coordinate, y coordinate, height, and width of the bounding box and the class probability score*

A bounding box can give us the following details:

Pc: Probability of having an object in the grid cell (0: no object, 1: an object).

Bx: If Pc is 1, it is the x coordinate of the bounding box.

By: If Pc is 1, it is the y coordinate of the bounding box.

Bh: If Pc is 1, it is the height of the bounding box.

Bw: If Pc is 1, it is the width of the bounding box.

C1: It is the class probability that the object belongs to Class 1.

C2: It is the class probability that the object belongs to Class 2.

Note   The number of classes depends on whether the problem at hand is a binary classification or a multilabel classification.

If an object lies over multiple grids, then the grid that contains the midpoint of that object is responsible for detecting that object.

Info   It is advisable to use a 19x19 grid as a general practice. Moreover, it is less probable that the midpoint of an object will lie in two separate grids.

So far, we are studying the approaches to determine the object; the next topic deals with measuring the performance of that detection which is the Intersection over Union.

5.6 Intersection over Union (IoU)

We have examined some of the methods for object detection. And in the subsequent sections, we will study Deep Learning architectures too. But still, we have to determine the accuracy of our predictions in object detection. Intersection over Union is a test to ascertain how close is our prediction to the actual truth.

It is represented by Equation 5-1 and is shown in Figure 5-4.

IoU = Overlapping region/Combined entire region   (Equation 5-1)

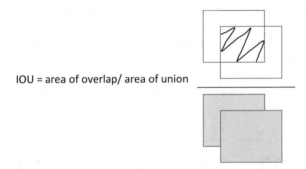

IOU = area of overlap/ area of union

Figure 5-4. *Intersection over Union is used to measure the performance of detection. The numerator is the common area, while the denominator is the complete union of the two areas. The higher the value of IoU, the better it is*

So, if we get a higher value of Intersection over Union, it means the overlap is better. Hence, the prediction is more accurate and better. It is depicted in the example in Figure 5-5 to visualize.

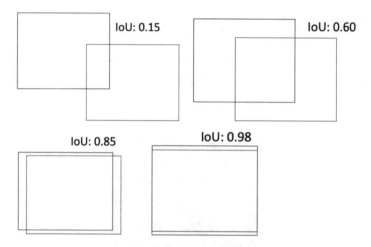

Figure 5-5. *IoU values for different positions of the overlapping blocks. If the value is closer to 1.0, it means that the detection is more accurate as compared to the value of 0.15*

As we can see in Figure 5-5, for IoU of 0.15, there is very less overlap between the two boxes as compared to 0.85 or 0.90. It means that the one with 0.85 IoU is a better solution to the one with 0.15 IoU. The detection solution can hence be compared directly.

Intersection over Union allows us to measure and compare the performance of various solutions. It also makes it easier for us to distinguish between useful bounding boxes and not-so-important ones. Intersection over Union is an important concept with wide usages. Using it, we can compare and contrast the acceptability of all the possible solutions and choose the best one from them.

We will now study non-max suppression techniques which are useful to filter significant bounding boxes.

5.7 Non-max suppression

When we are trying to detect an object in an image, we can have an object in multiple grids. It can be represented in Figure 5-6. And obviously, the grid with the highest probability will be the final prediction for that object.

Figure 5-6. *One object can be across multiple grids, and whichever gives the best result is the chosen grid to be used finally for detection purpose*

This entire process is done in the following steps:

1. Get the respective probabilities for all the grids.

2. Set a threshold for the probability and threshold for IoU.

3. Discard the ones which are below that threshold.

4. Choose the box with the best probability.

5.   Calculate the IoU of the remaining boxes.

6.   Discard the ones which are below the IoU threshold.

Using non-max suppression, we prune most of the bounding boxes which are below a certain level of threshold.

Info   Generally, the value is kept at 0.5. You are advised to iterate with different values to analyze the difference.

Hence, the important and significant ones are kept by the algorithm, while the noisier ones are removed. We will now proceed to anchor boxes, another important ingredient in object detection processes.

5.8 Anchor boxes

We wish to detect objects in Deep Learning, and we need a fast and accurate method to get the location and size of the object. An anchor box is a helpful concept for detecting objects.

Anchor boxes are used to capture the scaling and aspect ratio of the objects we wish to detect. They are of predefined size (height and width) and are sized based on the size of the object we want to detect. We are showing anchor boxes in Figure 5-7.

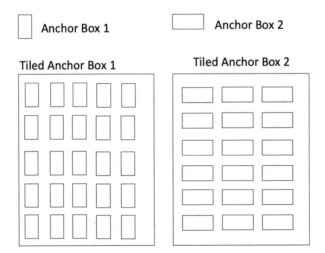

Figure 5-7. *Anchor boxes are used to capture the scaling and aspect ratio. We can tile the anchor boxes, and the Neural Network will output a unique set of predictions*

During the process of object detection, each anchor box is tiled across the image, and the Neural Network outputs a unique set of predictions for each of the anchor boxes. The output consists of the probability score, IoU, background, and offset for each anchor box. Based on the predictions made, the anchor boxes can be further refined.

We can have anchor boxes of multiple sizes to detect objects of different sizes. Using anchor boxes, we can detect objects of different scales. Even to the extent that multiple or overlapping objects can be detected using anchor boxes. It is surely a great improvement over sliding windows as we can now process the entire image in a single shot, making faster real-time object detection possible. To be noted is that the network does not predict the bounding boxes. The network predicts the probability scores and refinements for the tiled anchor box.

Now, we have studied the key components; now let's start with the Deep Learning architecture.

5.9 Deep Learning architectures

Deep Learning helps in object detection. We can detect objects of interest in an image or in a video or even in the live video stream. We are going to create a live video stream solution later in the chapter.

We have seen earlier that there are some problems with the sliding window approach. Objects can have different locations in an image and can be of different aspect ratio or size. An object might be covering the entire region; on the other hand, somewhere it will be covering a small percentage only. There might be more than one object present in the image. The objects can be at various angles or dimensions. Or one object can lie in multiple grids. And moreover, some use cases require real-time predictions. It results in having a very large number of regions and hence huge computation power. It will take a considerable amount of time too. The traditional approaches of image analysis and detection will not be of much help in such situations. Hence, we require Deep Learning–based solutions to resolve and develop robust solutions for object detection.

Deep Learning–based solutions allow us to train better and hence get better results. We are discussing the architectures now.

Let's start with R-CNN as the very first architecture!

5.9.1 Region-based CNN (R-CNN)

We understand that having a very large number of regions is a challenge. Ross Girshick et al. proposed R-CNN to address the problem of selecting a large number of regions. R-CNN is Region-based CNN architecture. Instead of classifying a huge number of regions, the solution suggests to use selective search and extract only 2000 regions from the image. They are called "Region Proposals."

The architecture for R-CNN is shown in Figure 5-8.

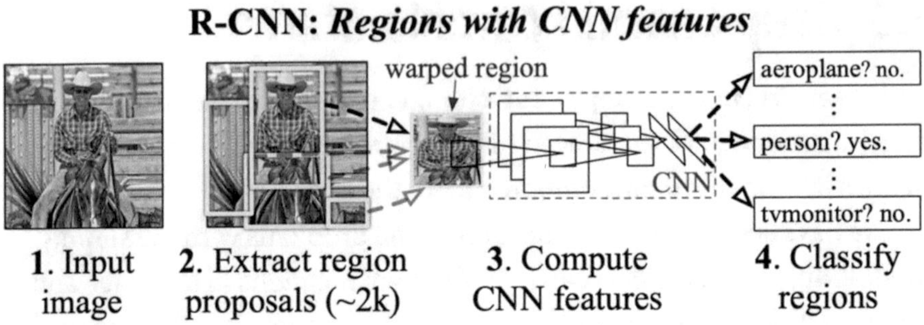

Figure 5-8. *The process in R-CNN. Here, we extract region proposals from the input image, compute the CNN features, and then classify the regions. Image source:* `https://arxiv.org/pdf/1311.2524.pdf` *and published here with the permission of the researchers*

With reference to Figure 5-8 where we have shown the process, let us understand the entire process in detail now:

1. The first step is to input an image, represented by step 1 in Figure 5-8.

2. Then get the regions we are interested in, which is shown in step 2 in Figure 5-8. These are the 2000 proposed regions. They are detected using the following steps:

   a) We create the initial segmentation for the image.

   b) Then we generate the various candidate regions for the image.

   c) We combine similar regions into larger ones iteratively. A greedy search approach is used for it.

   d) Finally, we use the generated regions to output the final region proposals.

3. Then in the next step, we reshape all the 2000 regions as per the implementation in the CNN.

4. We then pass through each region through CNN to get features for each region.

5. The extracted features are now passed through a support vector machine to classify the presence of objects in the region proposed.

6. And then, we predict the bounding boxes for the objects using bounding box regression. This means that we are making the final prediction about the image. As shown in the last step, we are making a prediction if the image is an airplane or a person or a TV monitor.

The preceding process is used by R-CNN to detect the objects in an image. It is surely an innovative architecture, and it proposes a region of interest as an impactful concept to detect objects.

But there are a few challenges with R-CNN, which are

1. R-CNN implements three algorithms (CNN for extracting the features, SVM for the classification of objects, and bounding box regression for getting the bounding boxes). It makes R-CNN solutions quite slow to be trained.

2. It extracts features using CNN for each image region. And the number of regions is 2000. It means if we have 1000 images, the number of features to be extracted is 1000 times 2000 which again makes it slower.

3.   Because of these reasons, it takes 40–50 seconds to make a prediction for an image, and hence it becomes a problem for huge datasets.

4.   Also, the selective search algorithm is fixed, and not much improvements can be made.

As R-CNN is not very fast and quite difficult to implement for huge datasets, the same authors proposed Fast R-CNN to overcome the issues. Let's understand the improvements suggested in the next section!

5.10 Fast R-CNN

In R-CNN, since we extract 2000 region proposals for an image, it is computationally a challenge to train or test the images. To tackle this issue, Ross Girshick et al. proposed that instead of executing CNN 2000 times for each image, we run it only once for an image and get all the regions of interest.

The architecture of the network is shown in Figure 5-9.

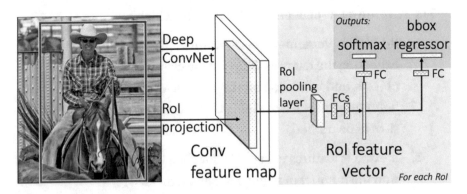

Figure 5-9. *The process in Faster R-CNN. We get the region of interest, and then we reshape all the inputs by applying a region of interest pooling layer. Then they are assessed by an FC layer, and finally softmax does the classification. Image source:* https://arxiv. org/pdf/1504.08083.pdf *and published here with the permission of the researchers*

The approach is similar to its predecessor barring the few changes:

1. The image is an input as shown in Figure 5-9.

2. The image is passed to the convolutional network which returns the respective regions of interest.

3. In the next step, we apply the region of interest pooling layer. It results in reshaping all the regions as per the input of the convolution. So it makes the size of all the regions of interest the same by applying the ROI pooling layer.

4. Now each of these regions is passed to the fully connected network.

5. Finally, the classification is done by the softmax layer. In parallel, the coordinates of the bounding boxes are identified using a bounding box regressor.

Fast R-CNN has a few advantages over R-CNN:

1. Fast R-CNN does not require feeding of 2000 region proposals to the CNN every time, and hence it is faster than R-CNN.

2. It uses only one convolution operation per image instead of three (extracting features, classification, and generating bounding boxes) used in the case of R-CNN. And hence there is no need to store a feature map, resulting in saving disk space.

3. Generally, softmax layers have better accuracy than SVM and have faster execution time.

The Fast R-CNN reduced the training time significantly and proved to be much more accurate too. But still the performance is not significantly fast enough due to the use of selective search as the proposed method to get the regions of interest. Hence, for a large dataset, the prediction is not fast enough. And that is why we have Faster R-CNN which we are discussing next.

5.11 Faster R-CNN

To overcome the slowness in R-CNN and Fast R-CNN, Shaoqing Ran et al. proposed Faster R-CNN. The intuition behind the Faster R-CNN is to replace the selective search which is slow and time-consuming. Faster R-CNN uses the Regional Proposal Network or RPN. The paper can be accessed at `https://papers.nips.cc/paper/2015/file/14bfa6bb14875e45bba028a21ed38046-Paper.pdf`

The architecture of Faster R-CNN is shown in Figure 5-10.

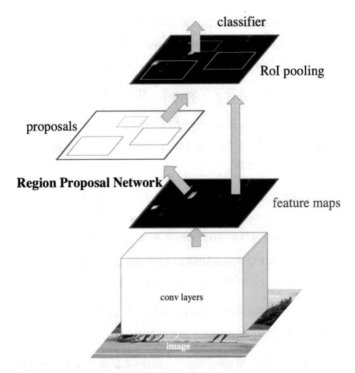

Figure 5-10. *Faster R-CNN is an improvement over the previous versions. It consists of two modules – one is a deep convolutional network, and the other is the Fast R-CNN detector*

To quote from the original paper at https://papers.nips.cc/
paper/2015/file/14bfa6bb14875e45bba028a21ed38046-Paper.pdf:

> *Our object detection system, called Faster R-CNN, is composed*
> *of two modules. The first module is a deep fully convolutional*
> *network that proposes regions, and the second module is the*
> *Fast R-CNN detector that uses the proposed regions. The entire*
> *system is a single, unified network for object detection.*

Let's dive deep into the architecture. The way a Faster R-CNN works is
as follows:

1. We take an input image and make it pass through
   CNN as shown in Figure 5-10.

2. From the feature maps received, we apply Region
   Proposal Networks (RPNs). The way an RPN works
   can be understood by referring to Figure 5-11.

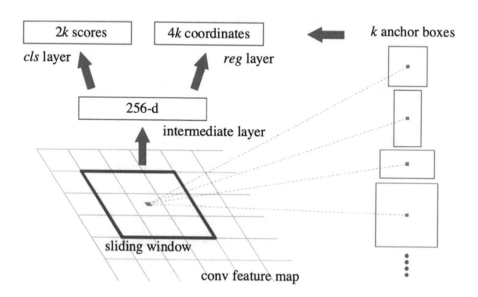

Figure 5-11. *Region proposal networks are used in Faster R-CNN.*
The image has been taken from the original paper

The substeps followed are

    a) RPN takes the feature maps generated from the last step.

    b) RPN applies a sliding window and generates k anchor boxes. We have discussed anchor boxes in the last section.

    c) The anchor boxes generated are of different shapes and sizes.

    d) RPN will also predict that an anchor is an object or not.

    e) It will also give the bounding box regressor to adjust the anchors.

    f) To be noted is RPN has not suggested the class of the object.

    g) We will get object proposals and the respective objectness scores.

3. Apply ROI pooling to make the size of all the proposals the same.

4. And then, finally, we feed them to the fully connected layers with softmax and linear regression.

5. We will receive the predicted Object Classification and respective bounding boxes.

Faster R-CNN is able to combine the intelligence and use deep convolution fully connected layers and Fast R-CNN using proposed regions. The entire solution is a single and unified solution for object detection.

Though Faster R-CNN is surely an improvement in terms of performance over R-CNN and Fast R-CNN, still the algorithm does not analyze all the parts of the image simultaneously. Instead, each and every part of the image is analyzed in a sequence. Hence, it requires a large number of passes over a single image to recognize all the objects. Moreover, since a lot of systems are working in a sequence, the performance of one depends on the performance of the preceding steps.

We will now proceed to one of the most famous algorithms – YOLO or You Only Look Once – in the next section.

5.12 You Only Look Once (YOLO)

You Only Look Once or YOLO is targeted for real-time object detection. The previous algorithms we discussed use regions to localize the objects in the image. Those algorithms look at a part of the image and not the complete image, whereas in YOLO a single CNN predicts both the bounding boxes and the respective class probabilities. YOLO was proposed in 2016 by Joseph Redmon, Santosh Divvala, Ross Girshick, and Ali Farhadi. The actual paper can be accessed at `https://arxiv.org/pdf/1506.02640v5.pdf`.

To quote from the actual paper, "We reframe object detection as a single regression problem, straight from image pixels to bounding box coordinates and class probabilities."

As shown in Figure 5-12, YOLO divides an image into a grid of cells (represented by S). Each of the cells predicts bounding boxes (represented by B). Then YOLO works on each bounding box and generates a confidence score about the goodness of the shape of the box. The class probability for the object is also predicted. Finally, the bounding box having class probability scores above are selected, and they are used to locate the object within that image.

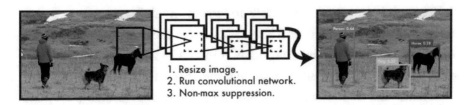

Figure 5-12. *The YOLO process is simple; the image has been taken from the original paper https://arxiv.org/pdf/1506.02640v5.pdf*

5.12.1 Salient features of YOLO

1. YOLO divides the input image into an SxS grid. To be noted is that each grid is responsible for predicting only one object. If the center of an object falls in a grid cell, that grid cell is responsible for detecting that object.

2. For each of the grid cells, it predicts boundary boxes (B). Each of the boundary boxes has five attributes – the x coordinate, y coordinate, width, height, and a confidence score. In other words, it has (x, y, w, h) and a score. This confidence score is the confidence of having an object inside the box. It also reflects the accuracy of the boundary box.

3. The width w and height h are normalized to the images' width and height. The x and y coordinates represent the center relative to the bound of the grid cells.

4. The confidence is defined as Probability(Object) times IoU. If there is no object, the confidence is zero. Else, the confidence is equal to the IoU between the predicted box and ground truth.

5. Each grid cell predicts C conditional class probabilities – Pr(Classi | Object). These probabilities are conditioned on the grid cell containing an object. We only predict one set of class probabilities per grid cell, regardless of the number of boxes B.

6. At the test time, we multiply the conditional class probabilities and the individual class predictions. It gives us the class-specific confidence scores for each box. It can be represented in Equation 5-2:

$$Pr(Class_i \mid Object) * Pr(Object) * IOU_{pred}^{truth}$$
$$= Pr(Class_i) * IOU_{pred}^{truth} \qquad \text{(Equation 5-2)}$$

We will now examine how we calculate the loss function in YOLO. It is important to get the loss function calculation function before we can study the entire architecture in detail.

5.12.2 Loss function in YOLO

We have seen in the last section that YOLO predicts multiple bounding boxes for each cell. And we choose the bounding box which has the maximum IoU with the ground truth. To calculate the loss, YOLO optimizes for sum-squared error in the output in the model as sum-squared error is easy to optimize.

The loss function is shown in Equation 5-3 and comprises localization loss, confidence loss, and classification loss. We are first representing the complete loss function and then describing the terms in detail.

$$\lambda_{coord} \sum_{i=0}^{S^2} \sum_{j=0}^{B} 1_{ij}^{obj} \left[(x_i - \hat{x}_i)^2 + (y_i - \hat{y}_i)^2 \right]$$

$$+ \lambda_{coord} \sum_{i=0}^{S^2} \sum_{j=0}^{B} 1_{ij}^{obj} \left[\left(\sqrt{w_i} - \sqrt{\hat{w}_i} \right)^2 + \left(\sqrt{h_i} - \sqrt{\hat{h}_i} \right)^2 \right]$$

Localization Loss

$$+ \sum_{i=0}^{S^2} \sum_{j=0}^{B} 1_{ij}^{obj} \left(C_i - \hat{C}_i \right)^2$$

Confidence Loss if an object is detected in the box

$$+ \lambda_{noobj} \sum_{i=0}^{S^2} \sum_{j=0}^{B} 1_{ij}^{noobj} \left(C_i - \hat{C}_i \right)^2$$

Confidence Loss if an object is not detected in the box

$$+ \sum_{i=0}^{S^2} 1_i^{obj} \sum_{c \in classes} (p_i(c) - \hat{p}_i(c))^2$$

Classification Loss

(Equation 5-3)

In Equation 5-3, we have localization loss, confidence loss, and classification loss, where $1^{obj}{}_i$ denotes if the object appears in cell i and $1^{obj}{}_{ij}$ denotes that the jth bounding box predictor in cell i is "responsible" for that prediction.

Let's describe the terms in the preceding equation. Here, we have

A. Localization loss is to measure the errors for the predicted boundary boxes. It measures their location and size errors. In the preceding equation, the first two terms represent the localization loss. $1^{obj}{}_i$ is 1 if the jth boundary box in cell i is responsible for detecting the object, else the value is 0. λ_{coord} is responsible for the increase in the weight for the loss in the coordinates of the boundary boxes. The default value of λ_{coord} is 5.

B. Confidence loss is the loss if an object is detected in the box. It is the second loss term in the equation shown. In the term earlier, we have

$\hat{C}_i$ is the box confidence score of the box j in cell i.

$1_{ij}^{obj} = 1$ if the j th boundary box in cell i is responsible for detecting the object, otherwise 0.

C.   The next term is a confidence loss if the object is not
      detected. In the term earlier, we have

$\mathbb{1}_{ij}^{noobj}$ is the complement of $\mathbb{1}_{ij}^{obj}$.

$\hat{C}_i$ is the box confidence score of the box j in cell i.

λ_{noobj} weights down the loss when detecting background.

D.   The final term is the classification loss. If an object is
      indeed detected, then for each cell it is the squared
      error of the class probabilities for each class.

$\mathbb{1}_{i}^{obj} = 1$ if an object appears in cell i, otherwise 0.

$\hat{p}_i(c)$ denotes the conditional class probability for class c in cell i.

The final loss is the sum total of all these components. As the objective
of any Deep Learning solution, the objective will be to minimize this loss
value.

Now we have understood the attributes of YOLO and the loss function;
we will now proceed to the actual architecture of YOLO.

5.12.3 YOLO architecture

The network design is shown in Figure 5-13 and is taken from the actual
paper at https://arxiv.org/pdf/1506.02640v5.pdf.

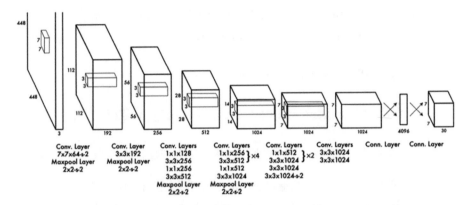

Figure 5-13.   *The complete YOLO architecture; the image has been taken from the original paper at* https://arxiv.org/pdf/1506.02640v5.pdf

In the paper, the authors have mentioned that the network has been an inspiration from GoogLeNet. The network has 24 convolutional layers followed by 2 fully connected layers. Instead of Inception modules used by GoogLeNet, YOLO uses 1x1 reduction layers followed by 3x3 convolutional layers. YOLO might detect the duplicates of the same object. For this, non-maximal suppression has been implemented. This removes the duplicate lower confidence score.

In Figure 5-14, we have a figure having 13x13 grids. In total, 169 grids are there wherein each grid predicts 5 bounding boxes. Hence, there are a total of 169*5 = 845 bounding boxes. When we apply a threshold of 30% or more, we get 3 bounding boxes as shown in Figure 5-14.

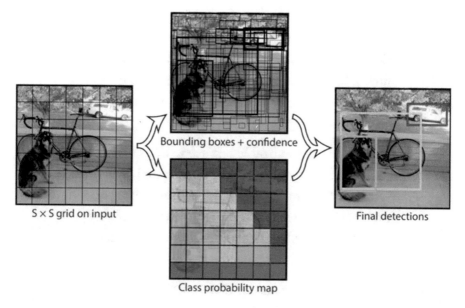

Figure 5-14. *The YOLO process divides the region into SxS grids. Each grid predicts five bounding boxes, and based on the threshold setting which is 30% here, we get the final three bounding boxes; the image has been taken from the original paper*

So, YOLO looks at the image only once but in a clever manner. It is a very fast algorithm for real-time processing. To quote from the original paper:

1.   YOLO is refreshingly simple.

2.   YOLO is extremely fast. Since we frame detection as a regression problem we don't need a complex pipeline. We simply run our Neural Network on a new image at test time to predict detections. Our base network runs at 45 frames per second with no batch processing on a Titan X GPU and a fast version runs at more than 150 fps. This means we can process streaming video in real-time with less than 25 milliseconds of latency. Furthermore, YOLO achieves more than twice the mean average precision of other real-time systems.

171

3. YOLO reasons globally about the image when making predictions. Unlike sliding window and region proposal-based techniques, YOLO sees the entire image during training and test time so it implicitly encodes contextual information about classes as well as their appearance.

4. YOLO learns generalizable representations of objects. When trained on natural images and tested on artwork, YOLO outperforms top detection methods like DPM and R-CNN by a wide margin. Since YOLO is highly generalizable it is less likely to break down when applied to new domains or unexpected inputs.

There are a few challenges with YOLO too. It suffers from high localization error. Moreover, since each of the grid cells predicts only two boxes and can have only one class as the output, YOLO can predict only a limited number of nearby objects. It suffers from a problem of low recall too. And hence in the next version of YOLOv2 and YOLOv3, these issues were addressed. Interested readers can get in-depth knowledge from the official website at `https://pjreddie.com/darknet/yolo/`.

YOLO is one of the most widely used object detection solutions. Its uniqueness lies in its simplicity and speed. The next Deep Learning architecture we will examine is a Single Shot MultiBox Detector or SSD in the next section.

5.13 Single Shot MultiBox Detector (SSD)

We have so far discussed R-CNN, Fast R-CNN, Faster R-CNN, and YOLO in the last sections. To overcome the slowness in the networks to work in real-time object detection, C. Szegedy et al. proposed the SSD (Single Shot MultiBox Detector) network in November 2016. The paper can be accessed at `https://arxiv.org/pdf/1512.02325.pdf`.

SSD uses the VGG16 architecture which we have discussed in the previous chapters but with a few modifications. By using an SSD, only a single shot is required to detect multiple images in an object. It is hence called *single* shot since it utilizes a *single* forward pass for both object localization and classification. Regional Proposal Network (RPN)–based solutions like R-CNN, Fast R-CNN, need two shots – first one to get the region proposals and second to detect the object for each proposal. And hence SSD proves to be much faster than RPN-based approaches. Szegedy et al. called it *multibox*, and the significance of the word detector is obvious. Let's explore more on the multibox detector concept.

Refer to Figure 5-15. We can say that after applying and passing through a series of convolutions, we obtain a feature layer of size m x n and p channels.

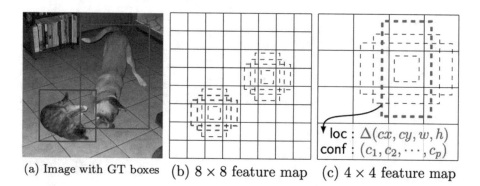

(a) Image with GT boxes   (b) 8×8 feature map   (c) 4×4 feature map

Figure 5-15. *SSD process is shown. We have an original image with ground truth (GT). 8x8 convolutions are done. We get different bounding boxes of sizes and location; the image has been taken from the original paper*

For each of the locations, we will get k bounding boxes which might be of varying sizes and aspect ratios. And for each of these k bounding boxes, we calculate c class scores and four offsets relative to the original default bounding box to finally receive (c+4)kmn outputs.

SSD implements a smooth L1 norm to calculate the location loss. It might not be as accurate as L1 but still be quite reasonably accurate.

More about multibox methods can be read at `https://arxiv.org/abs/1412.1441`.

The complete network is shown in Figure 5-16 as a comparison to YOLO. The image has been taken from the same paper with permission from the authors.

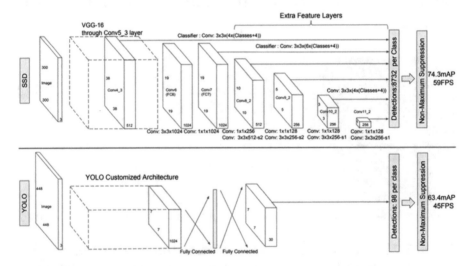

Figure 5-16. *A comparison of YOLO and SSD is shown here. The image is taken from the original paper at* `https://arxiv.org/pdf/1512.02325.pdf`

In SSD, different layers of feature maps are being passed through the 3x3 convolution layer to improve accuracy. If we analyze the preceding structure, we can observe that for the first layer of object detection (conv4_3), it has spatial dimensions of 38x38 which is quite a reduction in size, resulting in low accuracy for predicting smaller-sized objects. For the same conv4_3, we can calculate the output by using the formula in the discussion earlier. For conv4_3, the output will be 38x38x4x(c+4) where c is the number of classes to be predicted.

SSD uses two loss functions to calculate the loss – confidence loss (L_{conf}) and localization loss (L_{loc}). L_{conf} is the loss in making a class prediction, while L_{loc} is the mismatch between the ground truth and the predicted box. The mathematical formulas for both the losses are given in the previously mentioned paper, and their derivation is beyond the scope of the book.

There are a few other important processes followed in SSD:

1. Data augmentation by flipping, cropping, and color distortion is done to improve the accuracy. Each of the training examples is randomly sampled as follows:

    a. Utilize the original image.

    b. Sample a patch with IoU of 0.1, 0.3, 0.5, 0.7, or 0.9.

    c. Randomly sample a patch.

    d. The sampled patch has an aspect ratio between 0.5 and 2, and the size of each sampled patch is [0.1, 1] of the original size.

    Then each sampled image is resized to a fixed size and flipped horizontally. Photo distortions are also used for image augmentation.

2. SSD implements non-max suppression to remove the duplicate predictions. We have discussed non-max suppression at the start of this chapter.

3. SSD results in a higher number of predictions than the actual number of objects. We have more negative ones than the positive ones, resulting in class imbalance. To quote the actual paper: "Instead of using all the negative examples, we sort them using the highest confidence loss for each default box and pick the top ones so that the ratio between the negatives and positives is at most 3:1. We found that this leads to faster optimization and a more stable training."

Based on the preceding architecture, we can conclude a few points about SSD:

1. Detection of small-sized objects can be a challenge. To tackle this problem, we can increase the image resolution.

2. Accuracy is inversely proportional to speed; if we wish to increase the speed, we can increase the number of boundary boxes.

3. SSD has a higher classification error than R-CNN, but the localization error is lesser.

4. It makes good use of smaller convolution filters to predict the class and multiscale feature maps for detection. It helps in improving the accuracy.

5. To quote from the original paper: "The core of SSD is predicting category scores and box offsets for a fixed set of default bounding boxes using small convolutional filters applied to feature maps."

The accuracy of the SSD can be further improved. It confuses between objects with similar categories. And it is built on VGG16 which consumes a lot of training time. But SSD is a fantastic solution and can be easily used for end-to-end training. It is fast, can run in real time, and performs better than Faster R-CNN.

With this, we conclude the Deep Learning architectures for object detection. We have discussed the major algorithms, and in subsequent sections we will be developing actual Python code to implement the solution. But before that, we will examine the concept of Transfer Learning. It is an innovative solution which allows us to build on the state-of-the-art algorithms trained by the experts. Transfer learning is the next topic we are discussing.

5.14 Transfer Learning

As the name suggests, transfer learning is sharing the knowledge or transferring the learning to others. In the world of Deep Learning, researchers and organizations innovate and create novel Neural Network architectures. They use state-of-the-art capabilities of multicode powerful processors and train the algorithm on a large dataset carefully curated and chosen.

For us to create such an intelligence will be like reinventing the wheel. Hence, using transfer learning, we make use of those networks which have been trained on millions of data points. This allows us to use the intelligence generated by the researchers and implement the same on a real-world dataset. This process is referred to as *transfer learning*.

In transfer learning, we use a pre-trained model for our purpose. The pre-trained model has the final weights from the original model. The basic idea of using a pre-trained model is that the initial layers of the network detect the basic features, and as we move deeper, the features start to take shape. The basic feature extraction can be used for any type of images. So, if a model has been trained to distinguish between mobile phones, it can be used to distinguish between cars.

We can show the process in Figure 5-17. Here, the first layers of the network are frozen and will be used to extract the low-level features like edges, lines, and so on. And the last layers can be customized as per the business problem.

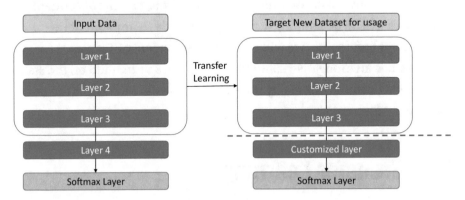

Figure 5-17. *Transfer learning utilizes the pre-trained network. The first layers are responsible for extracting the low-level features and are frozen. The last layers are customized for the problem at hand*

Transfer learning makes the learning faster than traditional machine learning and requires less training data. We will be discussing more details of the pre-trained model in Chapter 8.

Transfer learning is solving real-world business problems by leveraging the solutions developed in a different setting. We are going to use transfer learning now in the next section and in subsequent chapters of the book. In the previous chapters, we can employ transfer learning to use those networks.

Enough of theory, it's time to develop our Object Detection solutions. Time to hit the code!

5.15 Python implementation

We are going to implement real-time object detection using YOLO. The pre-trained weights have to be downloaded. The code, weights, labels, and the expected output can be downloaded from the GitHub repository link given at the start of the chapter.

Step 1: Import all the required libraries.

```
import cv2
from imutils.video import VideoStream
import os
import numpy as np
```

Step 2: Load the configurations from the local path. We are loading the weights, the configuration, and the labels. We are also setting the settings for the detection.

```
localPath_labels = "coco.names"
localPath_weights = "yolov3.weights"
localPath_config = "yolov3.cfg"
labels = open(localPath_labels).read().strip().split("\n")
scaling = 0.005
confidence_threshold = 0.5
nms_threshold = 0.005   # Non Maxima Supression Threshold Vlue
model = cv2.dnn.readNetFromDarknet(localPath_config, localPath_
weights)
```

Step 3: Now we are starting with the video in this step. We are then configuring for the layers which are unconnected by accessing from the object model.

```
cap = VideoStream(src=0).start()
layers_name = model.getLayerNames()
output_layer = [layers_name[i[0] - 1] for i in model.
getUnconnectedOutLayers()]
```

Note   You are advised to explore the components of the model and print them to understand better.

Step 4: Now we are ready to perform the detection of the objects. This step is the core step for the solution. It detects the object and the boundary boxes and adds the text on top of the box.

We are starting with a while loop at the start. Then we are reading the frame. In the next step, the width and height of the frame are being set up. Then we are going in a loop to iterate through each and every frame. If the confidence is above the confidence threshold we have set up earlier, the object will be detected.

We then label and the respective confidence scores for the object are shown in a box on the detected boundary boxes. The output is shown in Figure 5-18.

```
while True:
    frame = cap.read()
    (h, w) = frame.shape[:2]
    blob = cv2.dnn.blobFromImage(frame, 1 / 255.0, (416, 416),
    swapRB=True, crop=False)
    model.setInput(blob)
    nnoutputs = model.forward(output_layer)
    confidence_scores = []
    box_dimensions = []
    class_ids = []

    for output in nnoutputs:
        for detection in output:
            scores = detection[5:]
            class_id = np.argmax(scores)
            confidence = scores[class_id]
```

```
        if confidence > 0.5 :
            box = detection[0:4] * np.array([w, h, w, h])
            (center_x, center_y, width, height) = box.
            astype("int")
            x = int(center_x - (width / 2))
            y = int(center_y - (height / 2))
            box_dimensions.append([x, y, int(width),
            int(height)])
            confidence_scores.append(float(confidence))
            class_ids.append(class_id)
    ind = cv2.dnn.NMSBoxes(box_dimensions, confidence_scores,
    confidence_threshold, nms_threshold)
    for i in ind:
        i = i[0]
        (x, y, w, h) = (box_dimensions[i][0], box_dimensions[i]
        [1],box_dimensions[i][2], box_dimensions[i][3])
        cv2.rectangle(frame,(x, y), (x + w, y + h), (0, 255,
        255), 2)
        label = "{}: {:.4f}".format(labels[class_ids[i]],
        confidence_scores[i])
        cv2.putText(frame, label, (x, y - 5), cv2.FONT_HERSHEY_
        SIMPLEX, 0.5, (255,0,255), 2)
    cv2.imshow("Yolo", frame)
    if cv2.waitKey(1) & 0xFF == ord("q"):
        break
cv2.destroyAllWindows()
cap.stop()
```

The output has been shown in Figure 5-18. In real time, we are able to detect a cell phone with 99.79% accuracy.

Figure 5-18. *The real-time object detection is shown here. We are able to detect a cell phone with 99.79% accuracy*

In this solution, the real-world objects can be identified. And a bounding box is created around the object along with the name and confidence score.

This solution can be used for multiple use cases. The same code can be customized for datasets and can be used for detecting objects in images and videos too.

We can now proceed to the summary of the chapter.

5.16 Summary

Object detection is a very powerful solution. It is utilized at a number of domains and operations, and almost all the industries can be benefitted from object detection. It can be used for optical character recognition, autonomous driving, tracking objects and people, crowd surveillance, safety mechanisms, and so on. This computer vision technique is really changing the face of real-time capabilities.

In this chapter, we discussed object detection architectures – R-CNN, Fast R-CNN, Faster R-CNN, YOLO, and SSD. All of the networks are Deep Learning based and novel in design and architecture. Yet some outperform others. And generally there is a trade-off of speed and accuracy. So based on the business problem at hand, we have to carefully choose the network.

We also discussed transfer learning in this chapter. Transfer learning is a novel solution to use the pre-trained networks which have been trained on millions of images. Transfer learning allows us to use the intelligence generated by researchers and authors by using powerful processors. It is a tool which is enabling everyone to use these really deep networks and customize them as per the need. We used transfer learning to use the pre-trained YOLO to detect the object in real time. We are going to employ the transfer learning methodology moving ahead in other chapters.

Object detection can be in many practical solutions, but the input dataset defined the final accuracy of the solution. Hence, if you are using the networks for implementation on a custom dataset, be ready for some serious work in the data collection phase. The data will decide and define your success!

Now, in the next chapter, we are going to work on another exciting topic – face detection and recognition. Let's continue this journey!

You should be able to answer the questions in the exercise now!

REVIEW EXERCISES

You are advised to solve these questions:

1. What is the concept of anchor boxes and non-max suppression?

2. How are bounding boxes important for object detection?

3. How are R-CNN, Fast R-CNN, and Faster R-CNN different and what are the improvements?

4. How does Transfer Learning improve the Neural Network solution?

5. Download the Open Images 2019 dataset from www.kaggle. com/c/open-images-2019-object-detection and use it to create a solution using YOLO.

6. Download the chess dataset from https://public. roboflow.com/object-detection/chess-full and use it to locate the chess pieces based on the networks used in the chapter.

7. Get the racoon dataset from https://public.roboflow. com/object-detection/raccoon and use it to create an object detection solution.

8. Get the COCO dataset from https://cocodataset. org/#home and use it to compare the performance using different networks.

9. Download the Vehicles-OpenImages dataset from https:// public.roboflow.com/object-detection/vehicles-openimages and create an object detection solution.

5.16.1 Further readings

1. Explore the paper "The Object Detection Based on Deep Learning": https://ieeexplore.ieee.org/ document/8110383.

2. Explore the paper "MobileNets: Efficient Convolutional Neural Networks for Mobile Vision Applications": https://arxiv.org/ pdf/1704.04861v1.pdf.

3. Explore the paper "MobileNetV2: Inverted Residuals
    and Linear Bottlenecks": https://arxiv.org/
    pdf/1801.04381v4.pdf.

4. Explore the paper "Searching for MobileNetV3":
    https://arxiv.org/pdf/1905.02244v5.pdf.

CHAPTER 6

Face Recognition and Gesture Recognition

Who sees the human face correctly: the photographer,
the mirror, or the painter?

—Pablo Picasso

This chapter continues from the thought from Pablo Picasso. We humans are intrigued by our faces and faces of others, our smiles, our emotions, the different poses we make, and different expressions we have. Our mobile phones and cameras capture all of this. When we recognize a friend, we recognize the face – its shape, eyes, facial characteristics. And quite interestingly, even if we look at the same face from a side pose, we will be able to recognize it.

Surprisingly, we humans are able to detect the face even if we look at it after a long duration. We create that mental position of the attributes of a face, and we are able to recall it easily. At the same time, the gestures which we make using our hands are easily recognizable. Deep Learning is able to help recreate this capability. The usage of face recognition is

© Vaibhav Verdhan 2021
V. Verdhan, *Computer Vision Using Deep Learning*,
https://doi.org/10.1007/978-1-4842-6616-8_6

quite innovative – it can be used across domains of security, surveillance, automation, and customer experience – the use cases are many. There is a lot of research going on in this field.

This chapter attempts to teach the same magic to an algorithm.

In this chapter, we are going to study the following topics:

1. Face recognition

2. Process in face recognition

3. DeepFace architecture

4. FaceNet architecture

5. Python implementation for face recognition

6. Gesture recognition using OpenCV

So, let's continue our discussion!

6.1 Technical toolkit

The code and datasets for the chapter are uploaded at the GitHub link `https://github.com/Apress/computer-vision-using-deep-learning/tree/main/Chapter6` for this book. For this chapter, a GPU is good enough to execute the code, and you can use Google Colaboratory. We will be using the Python Jupyter Notebook.

Let's proceed with the Deep Learning architectures in the next section.

6.2 Face recognition

Face recognition is nothing new. We are born with a natural capability to differentiate and recognize faces. It is a trivial task for us. We can recognize the people we know in any kind of background, different lights, hair color, with cap or sunglasses, and so on. Even if a person has aged or has a beard, we can recognize them. Amazing!

Now we attempt to train the Deep Learning algorithms to achieve the same feat. A task so trivial and effortless for us is not an easy one for the machine. In Figure 6-1, we are having a face, then we are detecting a face, and then recognizing a face.

Vaibhav

Figure 6-1. *We have a face initially. In the second picture, a face is detected, and finally we are able to recognize a face with a specific name*

Recall in the last chapter we studied object detection. We can consider face recognition as a special case of object detection. Instead of discovering cars and cats, we are identifying people. But the problem is simpler; we have only the class of object to be detected – "face." But face detection is not the end state. We have to put a name to that face too, which is not trivial. Moreover, the face can be at any angle; a face can have different backgrounds. So, it is not an easy task. Also, we might be discovering faces in photographs or in videos. Deep Learning algorithms can help us in developing such capabilities. Deep Learning–based algorithms can leverage the computation power, advanced mathematical foundation, and the millions of data points or faces to train better models for face recognition.

Before we dive into the concepts and implementation of face recognition, we will explore the various use cases for this capability.

6.2.1 Applications of face recognition

Face recognition is a pretty exciting technology having applications across domains and processes. Some of the key uses are

1. Security management: The face recognition solutions are applicable for both online and offline security systems. Security services, police departments, and secret services utilize the power of machine learning–based face recognition techniques to trace the antisocial elements. Passport verification can happen quicker and in a much more robust fashion. Many countries do maintain a database of criminals' photographs which acts as a starting point to trace the culprits. The technology saves really a great deal of time and energy and allows the investigators to focus their energies on other areas.

2. Identity verification is another big area employing face recognition techniques. One of the most famous examples of ID verification is smartphones. Face ID is used in iPhones and the phone unlocks. Face recognition is being used by online channels and social media to check the identity of the person trying to access the account.

3. It is used by retailers to know when individuals with not-so-good history have entered the premises. When shoplifters, criminals, or fraudsters enter the stores, they act as a threat. Retailers can identify them and take immediate actions to prevent any crime.

4. Marketing becomes much sharper if the business knows the age, gender, and facial expressions of the customer. Giant screens can be installed (in fact have been done) to identify the target audience.

5. Consumer experience is improved when the consumer-product interaction is analyzed. Expressions of people when they touch the products or try them capture the real-world interactions. The data acts as a gold mine for the product teams to make necessary amendments to the product features. At the same time, the operations and in-store team can make the overall shopping experience more enjoyable and interesting.

6. Access to offices, airports, buildings, warehouses, and parking lots can be automated with no human intervention. A security camera takes a picture and compares it with the database to ensure authenticity.

The use cases discussed earlier are only a few of the many applications of face recognition capabilities. The solutions are hence broadly for face *authentication* or face *verification* or face *identification*. Many organizations and countries are creating huge databases of employees/individuals and investing to sharpen the skills further.

We will now proceed to examine the process of face recognition. It can be divided into step-by-step processes which we are discussing in the next section.

6.2.2 Process of face recognition

We click pictures from our phones and cameras. The photos are taken of various occasions – marriage, graduation, trips, holidays, conferences, and so on. When we upload the pictures on social media, it automatically detects the face and recognizes who the person is. An algorithm works in the background and does the magic. The algorithm is not only able to detect the face but will put a name to it from all the other faces in the background. We are studying the similar process in this section.

Broadly, we can have these four steps around face recognition as shown in Figure 6-2.

Figure 6-2. *Process followed in face detection – right from detection to recognition. We detect a face, perform alignment, extract the features, and finally recognize the face*

1. Face *detection* simply means to locate if there is a face or multiple faces in a photograph. And we will create a bounding box around it. Recall in Chapter 1, we did the same using OpenCV. It is shown in Figure 6-1 where we have detected the presence of a face in the photograph.

2. Once we have detected the face, we *normalize* the attributes of the face like the size and geometry. It is done so that it matches the facial database we have. We also reduce the effect of illumination, head movement, and so on.

3. Next, we *extract* the features from the face. Some of the distinguishing features are eyes, eyebrows, the nostrils, corners of the mouth, and so on.

4. And then we perform the face *recognition*. It means we match the face with the existing ones in the database. We might perform one of the two:

    a. Verify the given face with a known identity. In simple terms, we want to know "Is this Mr. X?". It is a case of one-to-one relationship.

    b. Or we might want to know "Who is this guy?," and in such a case we will have a one-to-many relationship.

The problem hence looks like a supervised learning classification problem.

In the first chapter, we created a face detection solution using OpenCV. There, we simply identified if there is a face present or not. Face recognition is giving a name to that face. It is imperative to note that without a concrete face detection, face recognition attempts will be futile. After all, first we should know if a face exists, then only we can give a name to that face. In other words, detection is to be done first followed by assigning a name. If there are more than one person in the photograph, we will be assigning names to all the faces detected in the photograph.

This is the entire process of face recognition. We will now study Deep Learning solutions for implementing the same.

6.2.2.1 Deep Learning modes for face recognition

Deep Learning is making its presence felt for face recognition too. Recall that face recognition is similar to any other image classification solution. But faces and attributes of features make face recognition and detection quite a special one.

We can use the standard Convolutional Neural Network for face recognition too. The layers of the network will behave and process the data similar to any other image analysis problem.

There are a plethora of solutions available, but the most famous are DeepFace, VGGFace, DeepID, and FaceNet as Deep Learning algorithms. We will study DeepFace and FaceNet in this chapter in depth and will create Python solutions using the same.

We will examine the DeepFace architecture now.

6.2.3 DeepFace solution by Facebook

DeepFace was proposed by researchers of Facebook AI Research (FAIR) in 2014. The actual paper can be accessed at `www.cs.toronto.edu/~ranzato/publications/taigman_cvpr14.pdf`.

Figure 6-3 shows the actual architecture of DeepFace, which is taken from the same paper mentioned previously.

Figure 2. **Outline of the *DeepFace* architecture**. A front-end of a single convolution-pooling-convolution filtering on the rectified input, followed by three locally-connected layers and two fully-connected layers. Colors illustrate feature maps produced at each layer. The net includes more than 120 million parameters, where more than 95% come from the local and fully connected layers.

Figure 6-3. *DeepFace architecture is shown here. The figure has been taken from the original paper at* `https://www.cs.toronto.edu/~ranzato/publications/taigman_cvpr14.pdf`

In the architecture shown earlier, we can analyze the various layers and the processes of the network. DeepFace expects an input image as a *3D-aligned* RGB image of 152x152. We will now explore this concept of 3D alignment in detail.

The objective of alignment is to generate a front face from the input image. The complete process is shown in Figure 6-4 which is taken from the same paper.

In the first step, we detect a face using six fiducial points. These six fiducial points are two eyes, tip of the nose, and three points on the lips. In Figure 6-4, it is depicted in step (a). This step detects the face in the image.

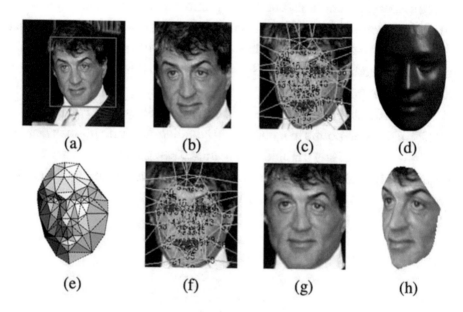

Figure 1. **Alignment pipeline.** (a) The detected face, with 6 initial fiducial points. (b) The induced 2D-aligned crop. (c) 67 fiducial points on the 2D-aligned crop with their corresponding Delaunay triangulation, we added triangles on the contour to avoid discontinuities. (d) The reference 3D shape transformed to the 2D-aligned crop image-plane. (e) Triangle visibility w.r.t. to the fitted 3D-2D camera; darker triangles are less visible. (f) The 67 fiducial points induced by the 3D model that are used to direct the piece-wise affine warpping. (g) The final frontalized crop. (h) A new view generated by the 3D model (not used in this paper).

Figure 6-4. *Face alignment process used in DeepFace. The image has been taken from the original paper. We should note how a face is progressively analyzed in steps*

In the second step, as shown in step (b), we crop and generate the 2D face from the original image. We should note how the face has been cropped from the original image in this step.

In the next steps, triangles are added on the contours to avoid discontinuities. We apply 67 fiducial points on the 2D-aligned crop with their corresponding Delaunay Triangulation. A 3D model is generated using a 2D to 3D generator, and the 67 points are plotted. It also allows us to align the out-of-plane rotation. Step (e) shows the visibility with respect to the fitted 2D-3D camera, and in step (f) we can observe the 67 fiducial points induced by the 3D model which are used to direct the piecewise affine wrapping.

We will discuss the Delaunay Triangulation briefly now. For a given set "P" of discrete points in a plane, in triangulation DT no point is inside the circumcircle of any triangle in Delaunay Triangulation. Hence, it maximizes the minimum angles of all the triangles in the triangulation. We are showing the phenomenon in Figure 6-5.

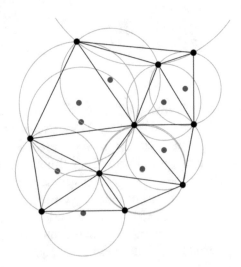

Figure 6-5. *Delaunay Triangulation. Image source:* https://commons.wikimedia.org/w/index.php?curid=18929097

Finally, we do a final frontalized crop. It is the final step which achieves the objective of 3D frontalization.

Once the step of 3D frontalization is done, then the image is ready to be fed to the next steps in the network. An image of 152x152 size is the input image which is fed to the next layer.

The next layer is the convolutional layer (C1) with 32 filters of size 11x11x3 followed by a 3x3 max pooling layer with a stride of 2. Then the next layer is another convolution with 16 filters and size 9x9x16.

Figure 2. **Outline of the *DeepFace* architecture**. A front-end of a single convolution-pooling-convolution filtering on the rectified input, followed by three locally-connected layers and two fully-connected layers. Colors illustrate feature maps produced at each layer. The net includes more than 120 million parameters, where more than 95% come from the local and fully connected layers.

Figure 6-6. *Complete DeepFace architecture is shown here. The image is from the original paper. We can observe that after frontalization has been done, the convolutional process is the next one*

And then we have three locally connected layers. We will discuss locally connected layers briefly as they are a bit different from fully connected layers.

Locally connected behave differently from fully connected layers. For a fully connected layer, each neuron of the first layer is connected to the next layer. For locally connected layers, we have different types of filter in a different feature map. For example, when we are classifying if the image is of a face, we can search for the mouth only at the bottom of the image. So locally connected layers are handy if we know that a feature should be restricted within a small space and there is no need to search for that feature across the entire image.

In DeepFace, we have locally connected layers, and hence we can improve the model as we can differentiate between facial regions based on different types of feature maps.

The penultimate layer is a fully connected layer which is used for face representation. The final layer is a softmax fully connected layer to do the classification.

The total number of parameters is 120 million. Dropout is being used as a regularization technique but is done only for the final fully connected layers. We also normalize the features between 0 and 1 and do an L2 normalization. The network generates quite sparse feature maps during the training, primarily since ReLU has been used as the activation function.

The validation was done on the LFW (Labeled Faces in the Wild) dataset and SFC dataset. LFW contains more than 13,000 web images of more than 5700 celebrities. SFC is the dataset by Facebook itself having ~4.4 million images of 4030 people each having 800 to 1200 facial images. The ROC curves for both the datasets are shown in Figure 6-7.

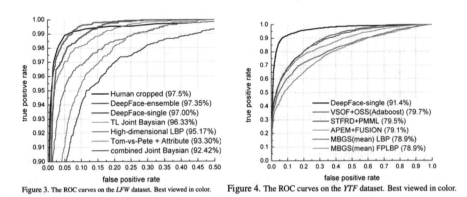

Figure 3. The ROC curves on the *LFW* dataset. Best viewed in color.   Figure 4. The ROC curves on the *YTF* dataset. Best viewed in color.

Figure 6-7. *ROC curve of LFW dataset and YTF dataset taken from the original paper at* https://www.cs.toronto.edu/~ranzato/ publications/taigman_cvpr14.pdf

DeepFace is one of the novel face recognition modes. It has more than 99.5% accuracy on the LFW dataset. It is able to resolve issues with pose, expression, or light intensity in the background. 3D alignment is quite a unique methodology which further enhances accuracy. The architecture has performed really well on LFW and YouTube Faces dataset (YTF).

We have finished discussing the DeepFace architecture now. We will now discuss the next architecture called FaceNet.

6.2.4 FaceNet for face recognition

In the last section, we studied DeepFace. Now we are examining a second architecture called FaceNet. It was proposed by Google researchers Florian Schroff, Dmitry Kalenichenko, and James Philbin in 2015. The original paper is "FaceNet: A Unified Embedding for Face Recognition and Clustering" and can be accessed at `https://arxiv.org/abs/1503.03832`.

FaceNet does not recommend a completely new set of algorithms or complex mathematical calculations to perform the face recognition tasks. The concept is rather simple.

All the images of faces are first represented in a Euclidean space. And then we calculate the similarity between faces by calculating the respective distances. Consider this, if we have an image, $Image_1$ of Mr. X, then all the images or faces of Mr. X will be closer to $Image_1$ rather than $Image_2$ of Mr. Y. The concept is shown in Figure 6-8.

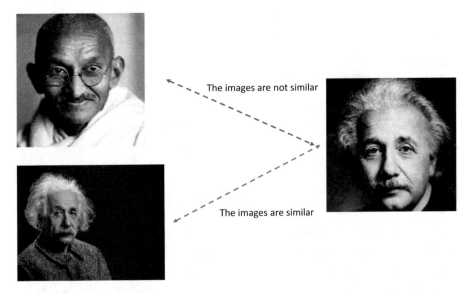

Figure 6-8. *The images of Einstein will be similar to each other, and hence the distance between them will be less, while the image of Gandhi will be at a distance*

The preceding concept is simpler to understand. We will understand the architecture in detail now. As shown in Figure 6-9, we can examine the complete architecture. The image has been taken from the original paper itself.

Figure 6-9. *FaceNet architecture. The image has been taken from the original paper at* https://arxiv.org/abs/1503.03832

The network starts with a batch input layer of the images. And then it is followed by a deep CNN architecture. The network utilizes an architecture like ZFNet or Inception network. We are discussing the Inception network in the next chapter of the book.

FaceNet implements 1x1 convolutions to decrease the number of parameters. 1x1 is again examined in detail in the next chapter. The output of these Deep Learning models is an embedding of images. L2 normalization is performed on the output. These embeddings are quite a useful addition. FaceNet understands the respective mappings from the facial images and then creates embeddings.

Once the embeddings are successfully done, we can simply go ahead, and with the help of newly created embeddings as the feature vector, we can use any standard machine learning technique. The usage of embeddings is the prime difference between FaceNet and other methodologies as other solutions generally implement customized layers for facial verifications.

The created embeddings are then fed to calculate the loss. As discussed earlier, the images are represented in a Euclidean space. The loss function aims to make the squared distance between two image embeddings of similar images small, whereas the squared distance between different images is large. In other words, the squared distance between the respective embeddings will decide the similarity between the faces.

There is one vital concept implemented in FaceNet – *triplet loss* function.

Triplet loss is shown in Figure 6-10; the image has been taken from the original paper itself.

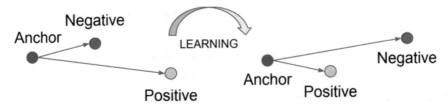

Figure 3. The **Triplet Loss** minimizes the distance between an *anchor* and a *positive*, both of which have the same identity, and maximizes the distance between the *anchor* and a *negative* of a different identity.

Figure 6-10. *Triplet loss used in FaceNet. The image has been taken from the original paper at* `https://arxiv.org/abs/1503.03832`

Triplet loss works on the concept we discussed in Figure 6-8 at the start of the FaceNet discussion. The intuition is that we want the images of the same person Mr. X closer to each other. Let us call that Image$_1$ as the anchor image. All the other images of Mr. X are called the positive images. The images of Mr. Y are referred to as negative images.

Hence, as per triplet loss, we want the distance between the embeddings of the anchor image and positive image to be less as compared to the distance between embeddings of the anchor image and negative image.

We would want to achieve Equation 6-1:

$$\left\| x_i^a - x_i^p \right\|_2^2 + \alpha < \left\| x_i^a - x_i^n \right\|_2^2, \forall \left(x_i^a, x_i^p, x_i^n \right) \in \tau . (1) \qquad \text{(Equation 6-1)}$$

where
Anchor image is x_i^a.
Positive image is x_i^p.
Negative image is x_i^n, so basically x_i is an image.
α is a margin that is enforced between positive and negative pairs. It is the threshold we set, and it signifies the difference between the respective pairs of images.

T is the set of all the possible triplets in the training set and has cardinality N.

Mathematically, triplet loss can be represented as in Equation 6-2. It is the loss which we wish to minimize.

$$\sum_{i}^{N}\left[\left\|f\left(x_{i}^{a}\right)-f\left(x_{i}^{p}\right)\right\|_{2}^{2}-\left\|f\left(x_{i}^{a}\right)-f\left(x_{i}^{n}\right)\right\|_{2}^{2}+\alpha\right]_{+}.(2) \qquad \text{(Equation 6-2)}$$

In the preceding equations, the embedding of an image is represented by f(x) such that $x \in \mathbb{R}$. It embeds an image x into a d-dimensional Euclidean space. $f(x_i)$ is the embedding of an image which is in the form of a vector of size 128.

The solution is dependent on the selection of the image pairs. There can be image pairs which the network will be able to pass. In other words, they will satisfy the condition of the loss. These image pairs might not add much to the learning and might also result in slow convergence.

For better results and faster convergence, we should select the triplets which do violate the condition in Equation 6-1.

Mathematically, for an anchor image x_i^a, we would want to select a positive image x_i^p such that the similarity is maximum and select a negative image x_i^n such that the similarity is minimum. In other words, we wish to have argmax $_{xip}$ || $f(x_i^a) - f(x_i^p)$ ||$_2^2$ which means given an anchor image x_i^a we wish to have a positive image x_i^p such that the distance is maximum.

Similarly, for a given anchor image x_i^a, we wish to get a negative image x_i^n such that the distance is minimum which is represented as argmin $_{xin}$ || $f(x_i^a) - f(x_i^n)$ ||$_2^2$.

Now, making this choice is not an easy task. During training, it is ensured that positive and negative are chosen as per the maximum and minimum functions given earlier on the mini-batch. SGD (Stochastic Gradient Descent) with Adagrad is used for training. The two networks which have been used are shown in the following (ZF-Net and Inception).

There are 140 million parameters in ZF-Net and 7.5 million parameters for Inception.

layer	size-in	size-out	kernel	param	FLPS
conv1	220×220×3	110×110×64	7×7×3, 2	9K	115M
pool1	110×110×64	55×55×64	3×3×64, 2	0	
rnorm1	55×55×64	55×55×64		0	
conv2a	55×55×64	55×55×64	1×1×64, 1	4K	13M
conv2	55×55×64	55×55×192	3×3×64, 1	111K	335M
rnorm2	55×55×192	55×55×192		0	
pool2	55×55×192	28×28×192	3×3×192, 2	0	
conv3a	28×28×192	28×28×192	1×1×192, 1	37K	29M
conv3	28×28×192	28×28×384	3×3×192, 1	664K	521M
pool3	28×28×384	14×14×384	3×3×384, 2	0	
conv4a	14×14×384	14×14×384	1×1×384, 1	148K	29M
conv4	14×14×384	14×14×256	3×3×384, 1	885K	173M
conv5a	14×14×256	14×14×256	1×1×256, 1	66K	13M
conv5	14×14×256	14×14×256	3×3×256, 1	590K	116M
conv6a	14×14×256	14×14×256	1×1×256, 1	66K	13M
conv6	14×14×256	14×14×256	3×3×256, 1	590K	116M
pool4	14×14×256	7×7×256	3×3×256, 2	0	
concat	7×7×256	7×7×256		0	
fc1	7×7×256	1×32×128	maxout p=2	103M	103M
fc2	1×32×128	1×32×128	maxout p=2	34M	34M
fc7128	1×32×128	1×1×128		524K	0.5M
L2	1×1×128	1×1×128		0	
total				140M	1.6B

Table 1. **NN1.**   This table show the structure of our Zeiler&Fergus [22] based model with 1×1 convolutions inspired by [9].   The input and output sizes are described in *rows* × *cols* × #*filters*.   The kernel is specified as *rows* × *cols*, *stride* and the maxout [6] pooling size as $p = 2$.

type	output size	depth	#1×1	#3×3 reduce	#3×3	#5×5 reduce	#5×5	pool proj (p)	params	FLOPS
conv1 (7×7×3, 2)	112×112×64	1							9K	119M
max pool + norm	56×56×64	0						m 3×3, 2		
inception (2)	56×56×192	2		64	192				115K	360M
norm + max pool	28×28×192	0						m 3×3, 2		
inception (3a)	28×28×256	2	64	96	128	16	32	m, 32p	164K	128M
inception (3b)	28×28×320	2	64	96	128	32	64	L_2, 64p	228K	179M
inception (3c)	14×14×640	2	0	128	256,2	32	64,2	m 3×3,2	398K	108M
inception (4a)	14×14×640	2	256	96	192	32	64	L_2, 128p	545K	107M
inception (4b)	14×14×640	2	224	112	224	32	64	L_2, 128p	595K	117M
inception (4c)	14×14×640	2	192	128	256	32	64	L_2, 128p	654K	128M
inception (4d)	14×14×640	2	160	144	288	32	64	L_2, 128p	722K	142M
inception (4e)	7×7×1024	2	0	160	256,2	64	128,2	m 3×3,2	717K	56M
inception (5a)	7×7×1024	2	384	192	384	48	128	L_2, 128p	1.6M	78M
inception (5b)	7×7×1024	2	384	192	384	48	128	m, 128p	1.6M	78M
avg pool	1×1×1024	0								
fully conn	1×1×128	1							131K	0.1M
L2 normalization	1×1×128	0								
total									7.5M	1.6B

Table 2. **NN2.** Details of the NN2 Inception incarnation. This model is almost identical to the one described in [16]. The two major differences are the use of L_2 pooling instead of max pooling (m), where specified. The pooling is always 3×3 (aside from the final average pooling) and in parallel to the convolutional modules inside each Inception module. If there is a dimensionality reduction after the pooling it is denoted with p. 1×1, 3×3, and 5×5 pooling are then concatenated to get the final output.

The model performed very well with 95.12% accuracy with standard error of 0.39 using the first 100 frames.

On the LFW dataset, quote from the paper:

Our model is evaluated in two modes: 1. Fixed center crop of the LFW provided thumbnail. 2. A proprietary face detector (similar to Picasa [3]) is run on the provided LFW thumbnails. If it fails to align the face (this happens for two images), the LFW alignment is used.

We achieve a classification accuracy of 98.87%±0.15 when using the fixed center crop described in (1) and the record breaking 99.63%±0.09 standard error of the mean when using the extra face alignment (2).

FaceNet is a novel solution as it directly learns an embedding into the Euclidean space for face verification. The model is robust enough to be not affected by the pose, lighting, occlusion, or age of the faces.

We will now look at the implementation of FaceNet using Python.

6.2.5 Python implementation using FaceNet

The code in this section is quite self-explanatory. We are using a pre-trained FaceNet model with its weights and calculating the Euclidean distance to measure the similarity between two faces. We are using the publicly available facenet_weights from `https://drive.google.com/file/d/1971Xk5RwedbudGgTIrGAL4F7Aifu7id1/view` by Sefik Ilkin Serengil. The model was converted from Tensorflow to Keras. The base model can be found at `https://github.com/davidsandberg/facenet`.

Step 1: Load the libraries.

```
from keras.models import model_from_json
from inception_resnet_v1 import *
import numpy as np

from keras.models import Sequential
from keras.models import load_model
from keras.models import model_from_json
from keras.layers.core import Dense, Activation
from keras.utils import np_utils

from keras.preprocessing.image import load_img, save_img, img_
to_array
from keras.applications.imagenet_utils import preprocess_input

import matplotlib.pyplot as plt
from keras.preprocessing import image
```

Step 2: Load the model now.

```
face_model = InceptionResNetV1()
face_model.load_weights('facenet_weights.h5')
```

Step 3: We will now define three functions – to normalize the dataset, to calculate the Euclidean distance, and to preprocess the dataset.

```
def normalize(x):
    return x / np.sqrt(np.sum(np.multiply(x, x)))

def getEuclideanDistance(source, validate):
    euclidean_dist = source - validate
    euclidean_dist = np.sum(np.multiply(euclidean_dist,
    euclidean_dist))
    euclidean_dist = np.sqrt(euclidean_dist)
    return euclidean_dist

def preprocess_data(image_path):
    image = load_img(image_path, target_size=(160, 160))
    image = img_to_array(image)
    image = np.expand_dims(image, axis=0)
    image = preprocess_input(image)
    return image
```

Step 4: Now we will calculate the similarity between the two images.

Here, we have taken these two images of a famous cricket celebrity – Sachin Tendulkar. These two images have been taken from the Internet.

```
img1_representation = normalize(face_model.predict(preprocess_
data('image_1.jpeg'))[0,:])
img2_representation = normalize(face_model.predict(preprocess_
data('image_2.jpeg'))[0,:])

euclidean_distance = getEuclideanDistance(img1_representation,
img2_representation)
```

The Euclidean distance similarity is 0.70. We can also implement a cosine similarity to test the similarity between two images.

We will now implement a gesture recognition solution using OpenCV in the next section.

6.2.6 Python solution for gesture recognition

Gesture recognition is one of the most innovative solutions which is helping humans talk to the system. Gesture recognition means that hand or face gestures can be captured by the system and a corresponding action can be taken by the system. It consists of detection, tracking, and recognition as the key components.

1. In detection, the visual part like the hand or a finger or a body part is extracted. The visual part should be within the view of the camera.

2. Then we track the visual part. It ensures that data is captured and analyzed frame by frame.

3. And finally, we recognize the gesture or a group of gestures. Based on the algorithm settings we have done, the training data used, the system will be able to identify the type of gesture that has been made.

Gesture recognition is quite a path-breaking solution and can be used in automation, medical devices, augmented reality, virtual reality, gaming, and so on. The use cases are many, and a lot of research is currently being done in this field.

In this book, we are going to implement a Finger Counting solution using OpenCV. The solution video can be accessed at www.linkedin. com/posts/vaibhavverdhan_counting-number-of-fingers-activity-64091765325767722944-Ln-R/.

Step 1: Import all the libraries here.

```
#   import all the necessary libraries
import cv2
import imutils
import numpy as np
from sklearn.metrics import pairwise

# global variables
bg = None
```

Step 2: We will now write a function to find the running average over the background.

```
#--------------------------------------------------------------
def run_avg(image, accumWeight):
    global bg
    # initialize the background
    if bg is None:
        bg = image.copy().astype("float")
        return

    # compute weighted average, accumulate it and update the
        background
    cv2.accumulateWeighted(image, bg, accumWeight)
```

Step 3: In this step, the segment function starts to segment the region of hand in the image.

```python
def segment(image, threshold=25):
    global bg
    # find the absolute difference between background and
      current frame
    diff = cv2.absdiff(bg.astype("uint8"), image)

    # threshold the diff image so that we get the foreground
    thresholded = cv2.threshold(diff, threshold, 255, cv2.
    THRESH_BINARY)[1]

    # get the contours in the thresholded image
    (_, cnts, _) = cv2.findContours(thresholded.copy(), cv2.
    RETR_EXTERNAL, cv2.CHAIN_APPROX_SIMPLE)

    # return None, if no contours detected
    if len(cnts) == 0:
        return
    else:
        # based on contour area, get the maximum contour which
          is the hand
        segmented = max(cnts, key=cv2.contourArea)
        return (thresholded, segmented)
```

Step 4: This code is used to count the number of fingers.

```python
from sklearn.metrics import pairwise
def count(thresholded, segmented):
    # find the convex hull of the segmented hand region
    chull = cv2.convexHull(segmented)

    # find the most extreme points in the convex hull
    extreme_top    = tuple(chull[chull[:, :, 1].argmin()][0])
```

```
extreme_bottom = tuple(chull[chull[:, :, 1].argmax()][0])
extreme_left   = tuple(chull[chull[:, :, 0].argmin()][0])
extreme_right  = tuple(chull[chull[:, :, 0].argmax()][0])

# find the center of the palm
cX = int((extreme_left[0] + extreme_right[0]) / 2)
cY = int((extreme_top[1] + extreme_bottom[1]) / 2)

# find the maximum euclidean distance between the center
  of the palm
# and the most extreme points of the convex hull
distance = pairwise.euclidean_distances([(cX, cY)],
Y=[extreme_left, extreme_right, extreme_top, extreme_
bottom])[0]
maximum_distance = distance[distance.argmax()]

# calculate the radius of the circle with 80% of the max
  euclidean distance obtained
radius = int(0.8 * maximum_distance)

# find the circumference of the circle
circumference = (2 * np.pi * radius)

# take out the circular region of interest which has
# the palm and the fingers
circular_roi = np.zeros(thresholded.shape[:2],
dtype="uint8")

# draw the circular ROI
cv2.circle(circular_roi, (cX, cY), radius, 255, 1)

# take bit-wise AND between thresholded hand using the
  circular ROI as the mask
# which gives the cuts obtained using mask on the
  thresholded hand image
```

```python
    circular_roi = cv2.bitwise_and(thresholded, thresholded,
    mask=circular_roi)

    # compute the contours in the circular ROI
    (_, cnts, _) = cv2.findContours(circular_roi.copy(), cv2.
    RETR_EXTERNAL, cv2.CHAIN_APPROX_NONE)

    # initalize the finger count
    count = 0

    # loop through the contours found
    for c in cnts:
        # compute the bounding box of the contour
        (x, y, w, h) = cv2.boundingRect(c)

        # increment the count of fingers only if -
        # 1. The contour region is not the wrist (bottom
          area)
        # 2. The number of points along the contour does not
          exceed
        #      20% of the circumference of the circular ROI
        if ((cY + (cY * 0.20)) > (y + h)) and ((circumference
        * 0.20) > c.shape[0]):
            count += 1

    return count
```

Step 5: The main function is given as follows:

```python
#----------------------------------------------------------------------
# Main function
#----------------------------------------------------------------------
if __name__ == "__main__":
    # initialize accumulated weight
    accumWeight = 0.5
```

```python
# get the reference to the webcam
camera = cv2.VideoCapture(0)

# region of interest (ROI) coordinates
top, right, bottom, left = 20, 450, 325, 690

# initialize num of frames
num_frames = 0

# calibration indicator
calibrated = False

# keep looping, until interrupted
while(True):
    # get the current frame
    (grabbed, frame) = camera.read()

    # resize the frame
    frame = imutils.resize(frame, width=700)

    # flip the frame so that it is not the mirror view
    frame = cv2.flip(frame, 1)

    # clone the frame
    clone = frame.copy()

    # get the height and width of the frame
    (height, width) = frame.shape[:2]

    # get the ROI
    roi = frame[top:bottom, right:left]

    # convert the roi to grayscale and blur it
    gray = cv2.cvtColor(roi, cv2.COLOR_BGR2GRAY)
    gray = cv2.GaussianBlur(gray, (7, 7), 0)
```

```
# to get the background, keep looking till a threshold
  is reached
# so that our weighted average model gets calibrated
if num_frames < 30:
    run_avg(gray, accumWeight)
    if num_frames == 1:
        print ("Calibration is in progress...")
    elif num_frames == 29:
        print ("Calibration is successful...")
else:
    # segment the hand region
    hand = segment(gray)

    # check whether hand region is segmented
    if hand is not None:
        # if yes, unpack the thresholded image and
        # segmented region
        (thresholded, segmented) = hand

        # draw the segmented region and display the
          frame
        cv2.drawContours(clone, [segmented + (right,
        top)], -1, (0, 0, 255))

        # count the number of fingers
        fingers = count(thresholded, segmented)

        cv2.putText(clone, str(fingers), (70, 45), cv2.
        FONT_HERSHEY_SIMPLEX, 1, (0,0,255), 2)

        # show the thresholded image
        cv2.imshow("Thesholded", thresholded)
```

```python
# draw the segmented hand
cv2.rectangle(clone, (left, top), (right, bottom),
(0,255,0), 2)

# increment the number of frames
num_frames += 1

# display the frame with segmented hand
cv2.imshow("Video Feed", clone)

# observe the keypress by the user
keypress = cv2.waitKey(1) & 0xFF

# if the user pressed "q", then stop looping
if keypress == ord("q"):
    break
```

Step 6: Now free up the memory.

```python
# free up memory
camera.release()
cv2.destroyAllWindows()
```

The output of this code will be a live video – a few screenshots are shown as follows.

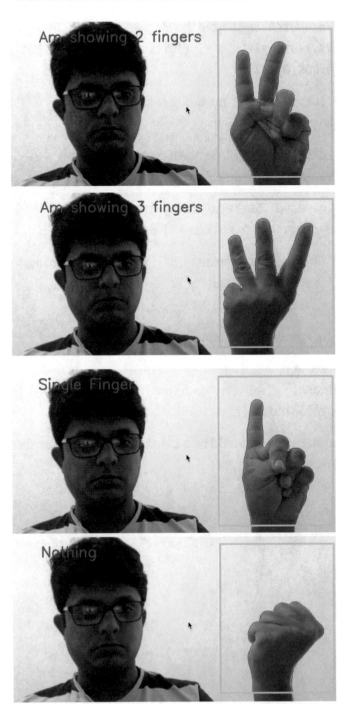

With this, we have created the face recognition and gesture recognition techniques using Deep Learning and OpenCV. We will now proceed to the summary of this chapter.

6.3 Summary

Face detection and recognition are an intriguing field. Facial attributes are quite unique. A capability which is quite easy for humans is difficult to be taught to machines. There are a great many uses of detecting faces which we have discussed in detail in this chapter. They are utilized in a number of domains and are very intuitive to understand. Deep Learning is helping us achieve it. The road is still very long, and we have to improve a lot in this journey. With better machines and sophisticated algorithms, the improvements are always on the cards.

At the same time, it is imperative that the facial dataset captured is clean, representative, and complete. If there is a lot of background noise in the image, or the images are blurred or have any other defect, it will be really a difficulty to train the network.

There are other extensions which can be done to facial and gesture recognition. Age detection, gender detection, and emotion detection are a few which are already in progress and developed across organizations and research institutes.

In this chapter, we studied face recognition methods and Deep Learning architectures for the same. We examined DeepFace and FaceNet in this chapter and created a Python solution using a pre-trained network. We also created a gesture recognition solution using OpenCV.

The next chapter deals with another interesting area of computer vision – video analytics. In the next chapter, we also study ResNet and Inception networks which are state-of-the-art algorithms. So, stay tuned!

You may now proceed to the questions.

REVIEW EXERCISES

1. What are the various processes in face recognition systems?

2. What is the concept of facial alignment?

3. What is the concept of triplet loss?

4. What are the various use cases of gesture recognition?

5. Download the Tufts dataset from www.kaggle.com/
    kpvisionlab/tufts-face-database and develop a face
    recognition system by working on it.

6. Download the Google facial expression comparison dataset
    from https://research.google/tools/datasets/
    google-facial-expression/ and develop a system to
    analyze facial expressions.

7. Download the Labeled Faces in the Wild dataset from
    http://vis-www.cs.umass.edu/lfw/ and create a facial
    verification solution using FaceNet and DeepFace.

8. Download the YouTube Faces dataset with Facial Keypoints
    from www.kaggle.com/selfishgene/youtube-faces-
    with-facial-keypoints and use it to recognize faces in
    unconstrained videos. If required, concepts of video analytics
    can be studied in the next chapter.

6.3.1 Further readings

1. Go through the paper "A Dataset and Benchmark for Large-scale Multi-modal Face Anti-spoofing" at https://arxiv.org/pdf/1812.00408v3.pdf.

2. Go through the paper "Probabilistic Face Embeddings" at https://arxiv.org/pdf/1904.09658.pdf.

3. Go through the paper "VGGFace2: A dataset for recognising faces across pose and age" at https://arxiv.org/pdf/1710.08092v2.pdf.

4. Go through the paper "The Devil of Face Recognition is in the Noise" at https://arxiv.org/pdf/1807.11649v1.pdf.

CHAPTER 7

Video Analytics Using Deep Learning

A minute of video is worth 1.8 million words.

—Dr. James McQuivey

Videos are a really powerful medium. Roughly 300 hours of videos are uploaded to YouTube every minute. And the number of videos created is increasing daily. With the advent of smartphones and improved hardware, the video quality is enhanced. More videos are being created and stored across domains and geographies. We have movies, advertisements, short clips, and personal videos. Most of the videos contain human faces, objects, and some movements of objects. A video might be shot during the daytime or in the night, under different lighting conditions. We have cameras capturing the movement of pedestrians on the road, manufacturing cameras for monitoring goods and products on manufacturing lines, security cameras for surveillance on airports, and number plate detection and reading systems in the parking lots, to name a few of the video analytics solutions.

This chapter enhances the capabilities we have developed from images to videos. The algorithms which have been used to classify images and detect objects are extended to videos. After all, in simple terms, a video is a sequence of images. We will develop solutions on videos using Python as we have done in the previous chapters.

© Vaibhav Verdhan 2021
V. Verdhan, *Computer Vision Using Deep Learning*,
https://doi.org/10.1007/978-1-4842-6616-8_7

In this chapter, we are also extending our knowledge to ResNet and Inception network architectures. Both of the networks are advanced networks and most sought after for a lot of cutting-edge Deep Learning solutions. With the inclusion of ResNet and Inception networks, we would have covered the complete networks we wish to study in this book.

In this chapter, we are going to study the following topics:

1. ResNet architecture

2. Inception architecture and its versions

3. Video analytics and its use cases

4. Python implementation using ResNet, Inception v3 for video

5. Summary

All the very best for this chapter!

7.1 Technical toolkit

There is no change in the technical stack required, and we continue to use the similar settings.

We are using the Python Jupyter Notebook. The code for this chapter along with the dataset has been checked into the git repo at `https://github.com/Apress/computer-vision-using-deep-learning/tree/main/Chapter7`.

7.2 Video processing

Videos are not new to us. We record videos using our phone, laptops, hand cameras, and so on. YouTube is one of the biggest sources of videos. Advertisements, movies, sports, social media uploads, TikTok videos, and so on are getting created every second. And by analyzing them, we can uncover a lot of insights about the behavior, interactions, timings, and sequence of things. A very powerful medium indeed!

There can be multiple approaches to design a video analytics solution. We can consider video as a collection of frames and then perform analytics by treating the frames as individual images. Or we can also add an additional dimension of sound to it. In this book, we are concentrating our efforts on images alone, and sound is not included.

We will now explore the various use cases of video analytics in the next section.

7.3 Use cases of video analytics

Videos are a rich source of knowledge and information. We can utilize Deep Learning–based capabilities across domains and business functions. Some of them are listed as follows:

1. Real-time face detection can be done using video analytics, allowing us to detect and recognize the faces. It has huge benefits and applications across multiple domains. We have discussed the application in detail in the last chapter.

2. In disaster management, video analytics can play a significant role. Consider this. In a flood-like situation, by analyzing videos of the actual area, the rescue team can identify the zones they should concentrate on. It will help reduce the time to action which directly leads to more lives saved.

3. Similarly, for crowd management, video analytics plays an important role. We can identify the concentration of the population and the eminent dangers in that situation. The respective team can analyze the videos or a real-time streaming of video using cameras. And a suitable action can be taken to prevent any mishappening.

4. By analyzing the social media videos, the marketing teams can improve the contents. The marketing teams can even analyze the contents of the competitors and tweak their business plan accordingly as per the business needs.

5. For object detection and object tracking, video analytics can quickly come up with a decision if an object is present in the video or not. This can save manual efforts. For example, if we have a collection of videos of different cars and we wish to classify them in different brands, the manual process will be to open each and every video and then take a decision – which is both time-consuming and error-prone. Using Deep Learning–based video classification, this entire process can be automated.

6. Video analytics can help in the inspection and quality assurance. Instead of manual inspection of each part present in a machine, a video can be taken for the entire process. And then using Deep Learning, the quality inspection can be conducted.

These are not the only use cases. There are a number of applications across domains and sectors. With Deep Learning–based solutions, video analytics is really making an impact into the business world.

Before we proceed with video analytics, we will first study a challenge which very deep networks face – *vanishing gradient* problem. Then we will examine two very powerful Deep Learning architectures – ResNet and Inception. We are starting with the vanishing gradient problem in the next section.

7.4 Vanishing gradient and exploding gradient problem

The Neural Networks are trained using backpropagation and gradient-based learning methods. During training, we want to reach the most optimum value of weights resulting in minimum loss. Now, each of the weights constantly gets updated during the training of the algorithm. The update is proportional to the partial derivative of the error function with respect to the current weight in each training iteration. We have examined the concept in Chapter 2. In Figure 7-1, we are showing that in the sigmoid function, we can face the problem of vanishing gradient, while in the case of a ReLU or Leaky ReLU, we will not have vanishing gradient as an issue.

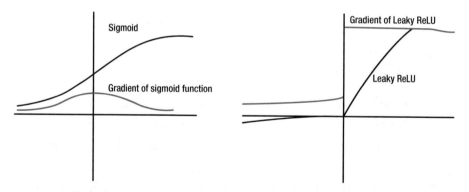

Figure 7-1. *Vanishing gradient is a challenge we face with deep Neural Networks. The figure on the left shows that for the sigmoid activation function, we do face a big problem which gets sorted for Leaky ReLU*

The challenge can be sometimes this update becomes too small, and hence the weight does not get updated. It results in very less or practically no training of the network. This is referred to as the vanishing gradient problem.

Let's understand the problem in depth now. We are again looking at the basic network architecture in Figure 7-2.

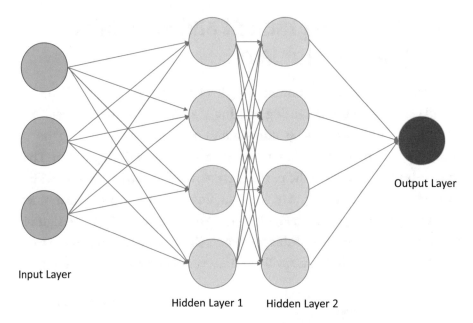

Figure 7-2. *Basic neural architecture having an input layer, hidden layers, and an output layer*

We know that each of the neurons in the network has an activation function and a bias term. It accepts a finite number of input weight products, adds a bias term to it, and then the activation function is applied on it. The output is then passed to the next neuron.

We also know that in a network, the difference between the expected output and the predicted value is calculated which is nothing but the error term. We would want the error term to be minimized. The error will be minimized when we have achieved the best combination of weights and biases across the layers and neurons which minimizes the error.

When the error is calculated, a gradient descent is applied on the graph of the error function. This gradient descent is the differentiation of the error function with respect to each of the independent variables (weights and biases) present in it. This is the job of the backpropagation algorithm – which takes care of manipulating these weights and biases by a constant term called the learning rate. This is done from the last layer to the first layer in the backward direction or from the right to the left. In each successive iteration, gradient descent is calculated and the direction of change is determined. And hence, the weights and biases are updated till the network minimizes the error – or, in other words, till the error reaches a *global minima* as shown in Figure 7-3. The error gradient hence is the direction and magnitude calculated during the training of the network. It is used to update the weights in the right direction and right magnitude.

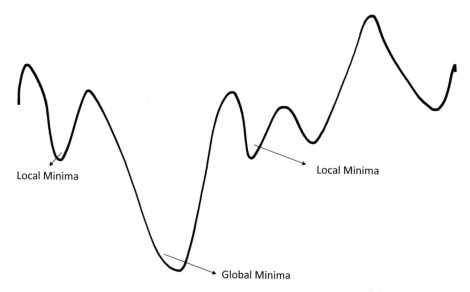

Local Minima

Local Minima

Global Minima

Figure 7-3. *To minimize the loss, we would want to reach the global minima of a function. Sometimes, we might not be able to minimize the loss and can be stuck at the local minima*

Now a situation arises wherein if we have a very deep network, the initial layers have a very less impact on the final output as compared to the final layers of the network. Or in other words, the initial layers undergo very less training, and their values undergo very less amount of change. This is due to the fact that the backpropagation computes the gradients using a chain rule from the final layers to the initial layers. Hence, in an n-layered network, the gradient decreases exponentially with the value of n, and hence the initial layers will train very slowly. Or, in the worst-case scenario, they will stop to train.

There can be multiple signs to check for the vanishing gradient problem:

1. The easiest way to detect vanishing gradient is through kernel weight distribution. If the weights are dying to zero or very very close to zero, we might be encountering a vanishing gradient problem.

2. The model's weight close to the final layers will have more change as compared to the initial layers.

3. The model will not improve or will improve very slowly during the training phase.

4. Sometimes, the training stops early. It means that any further training does not improve the model.

There are a few suggested solutions for the vanishing gradient problem:

1. Generally, reducing the number of layers in the network might help in resolving gradient problems. But at the same time, if the number of layers is reduced, the network's complexity goes down, and it can also impact the performance of the network.

2. The ReLU activation function resolves the vanishing gradient problem. ReLU suffers less from vanishing gradients as compared to tanh or sigmoid activation functions.

3. Residual networks or ResNets are also one of the solutions for this problem. They do not resolve the problem by saving the gradient flow; instead, they use a combination or ensemble of multiple smaller

networks. And hence, ResNets despite being deep networks are able to achieve lesser loss as compared to shallow networks.

On one hand, we have a vanishing gradient problem, while on the other hand, we have an exploding gradient problem.

In deep networks, error gradients sometimes become very large as they get accumulated. Hence, the updates in the networks will be very large which make the network unstable. There are a few signs of exploding gradients which can help us in detecting exploding gradient:

1. The model is suffering from poor loss during the training phase.

2. During the training of the algorithm, we might encounter NaN for the loss or for the weights.

3. The model is generally unstable, or in other words the updates to loss in subsequent iterations are huge indicating an unstable state.

4. The error gradients are constantly above 1 for each of the layers and neurons in the network.

Exploding gradient can be resolved using

1. We can reduce the number of layers in the network or can try reducing the batch size during training.

2. L1 and L2 weight regularization can be added which will act as a penalty to the network loss functions.

3. *Gradient clipping* is one of the methods which can be used. We can limit the size of the gradients during the process of training. We set a threshold for the error gradients, and the error gradients are set to that limit or *clipped* if the error gradient exceeds the threshold.

4. We can use LSTM (long short-term memory) if we
    are working with Recurrent Neural Networks. This
    concept is beyond the scope of this book.

Both vanishing and exploding gradients are a nuisance which will
impact the performance of the network. They can make the network
unstable and require correction using a few of the options mentioned
earlier. Now we are clear with vanishing gradients, we will study the ResNet
architecture in detail in the next section.

7.5 ResNet architecture

We have studied a lot of architectures in the last chapters. We have used
them for image classification, object detection, face recognition, and so
on. They are deep Neural Networks and generating good results for us. But
in very deep networks, we encounter a problem of vanishing gradients.
Residual networks or *ResNets* solve this problem by using skip connections.
ResNets were invented by Kaiming He, Xiangyu Zhang, Shaoqing Ren, and
Jian Sun, and the paper was presented in Dec 2015. More details can be
found at `https://arxiv.org/pdf/1512.03385.pdf`.

Skip connections take the activation from one layer to a much deeper
layer in the network which allows us to train even more deep networks,
which may be beyond 100 layers. Now, we will discuss ResNet and skip
connection in detail in the next section.

7.5.1 ResNet and skip connection

When we talk about Neural Networks and the fantastic performance
shown by them, immediately it is attributed to the *depth* of the network. It
is assumed that the deeper the network is, the better is the accuracy. The
initial layers will learn the basic features, and deeper layers will learn more
advanced features.

But it was found, by adding a greater number of layers, we are increasing the complexity of the network. In fact for a deeper network (like 56 layers deep), the loss was greater than a network with less (20) layers.

Note   Generally, models using convolutional and fully connected layers between 16 and 30 give the best results for CNN.

This loss can be attributed to the problem of vanishing gradients we discussed earlier. To resolve the problem of vanishing gradient, residual blocks are introduced as shown in Figure 7-4. Residual blocks implement *skip connection* or identity mapping.

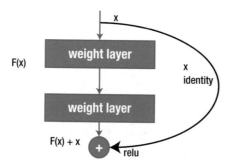

Figure 7-4. *Skip connection is the heart of residual networks or ResNets. Note how the output from the previous layer is passed to the next layer, thereby skipping a layer in between. It allows training deeper networks without the problem of vanishing gradients*

This identity mapping has no input parameters of itself; rather, it takes the output from the previous layer and adds to the next layer. In other words, it acts as a shortcut connection before the second activation. Because of this shortcut, it is possible to train even deeper networks without diluting the performance of the network. This is the heart of the solution and the reason for its resounding success.

We are now examining the ResNet-34 architecture in detail in Figure 7-5. The original architecture is taken from the link of the paper: `https://arxiv.org/pdf/1512.03385.pdf`.

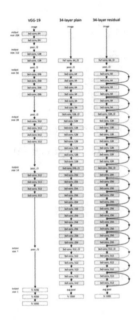

- This is the architecture of ResNet 34
- No fully connected layers and no dropouts were used
- All the convolutions are 3x3
- The dotted lines represent where the dimensions are different.
- To solve the difference in dimensions, the input is down-sample by 2 and then zero padding to match the two dimensions.

Figure 7-5. *ResNet-34 complete architecture – in the middle is a plain network without skip connections, while on the right a network with residual connections is shown. The architecture has been taken from the original paper at* `https://arxiv.org/pdf/1512.03385.pdf`

Let's go a bit deeper into the network. Observe the four residual blocks in the architecture as shown in Figure 7-6.

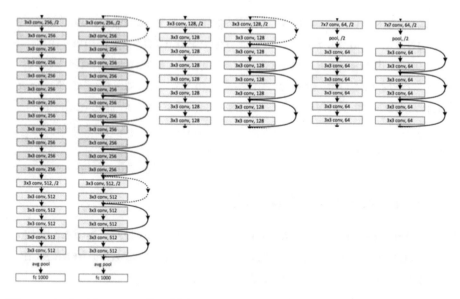

Figure 7-6. *Four residual blocks are shown in the figure. Note how for each of the plain networks on the left, we have a corresponding block using skip connection. Skip connections are allowed to train deeper networks without an adverse impact on the accuracy of the network. For example, for the very first block, we have a plain network having a 7x7 conv layer followed by a 3x3 conv layer. Note the corresponding block using the skip connection*

We can analyze that in each residual architecture, skip connection takes the output from the previous layer and shares it two blocks away. This is the core difference with the plain architecture on the left, which boosts the performance for ResNet.

Skip connections extend the capabilities of deep networks in a very interesting manner. The inventors tested the network with 100 and 1000 layers on the CIFAR dataset. The inventors found that using an ensemble of residual networks was able to achieve a 3.57% error rate on ImageNet and hence secured first place in the ILSVRC2015 competition.

There are other variants of ResNet gaining popularity like ResNetXt, DenseNet, and so on. These variants explore the changes which can be made to the original ResNet architecture. For example, ResNetXt introduced *cardinality* as one of hyperparameters for the model. We have listed research papers at the end of the chapter for interested audiences.

We will now understand another innovative architecture called the Inception network.

7.5.2 Inception network

Deep Learning is fantastic when it comes to complex tasks. And we have observed that using stacked convolutional layers, we are able to train deep networks. But there are a few challenges with it:

1. Networks become overcomplicated and demand huge computation power.

2. Vanishing and exploding gradient problems are encountered while training the network.

3. Many times, while observing the training and test accuracy, networks overfit and hence are not useful for unseen datasets.

4. Moreover, choosing the best kernel size is a tough decision. A poorly chosen kernel size will lead to ill-fitting results.

To resolve the challenges faced, the researchers thought that why can't we go *wide* rather than going *deep*. More technically, have filters with multiple sizes operate at the same level. And hence Szegedy et al. proposed the *Inception module.* The complete paper can be accessed here: https://arxiv.org/pdf/1409.4842v1.pdf.

Figure 7-7 represents two versions of the Inception module presented in the same paper.

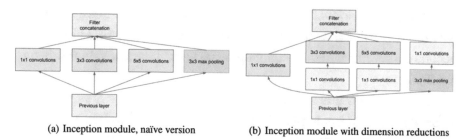

(a) Inception module, naïve version   (b) Inception module with dimension reductions

Figure 7-7. *On the left, we have the naïve version of the Inception module. In the naïve version, we have 1x1, 3x3, and 5x5 convolutions. To reduce the computation, the researchers added a 1x1 conv layer for dimensionality reduction. The image has been taken from https:// arxiv.org/pdf/1409.4842v1.pdf*

In the first version, a naïve version of Inception, three different sizes of convolution were done – 1x1, 3x3, and 5x5. Additionally, a max pooling of 3x3 was also proposed. All the respective outputs are then stacked and fed to the next Inception module.

But as the computation cost increases, the researchers added an additional 1x1 convolutional layer for dimensionality reduction. This limits the number of input channels, and 1x1 is less computationally expensive than 3x3 or 5x5. A salient feature is the 1x1 convolution is after the max pooling layer.

Using this second version of dimensionality reduction, a full network was created which is known as *GoogLeNet*. The researchers chose the name as an homage to Yann LeCuns pioneering the LeNet-5 architecture.

Before we go deep into studying the GoogLeNet architecture, it is imperative to discuss the uniqueness of 1x1 convolutions.

7.5.2.1 1x1 convolutions

In deep networks, the number of feature maps increases with the depth of the network. So, if an input image has three channels and a 5x5 filter has to be applied, then a 5x5 filter will be applied in blocks of 5x5x3. Moreover,

235

if the input is a block of feature maps from another convolution layer having a depth of 64, then a 5x5 filter will be applied in 5x5x64 blocks. It becomes a computationally challenging task. 1x1 filters help in resolving this challenge.

1x1 convolutions are also called *network-in-network*. It is very simple to understand and implement. It has a single feature or weight of each channel in the input. Similar to any other filter, the output is also a single number. It can be used anywhere in the network, does not require any padding, and generates feature maps with exactly the same width and height as the input.

If the number of channels in the 1x1 convolution is the same as the number of channels in the input image, then invariably the output will also contain the same number of 1x1 filters. And there, 1x1 acts as a nonlinearity function. It is shown in Figure 7-8.

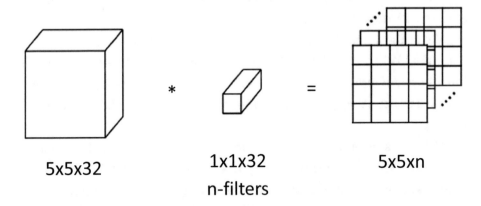

5x5x32   1x1x32   5x5xn
                n-filters

Figure 7-8. *1x1 convolutional layer is used to shrink the number of channels. Here, the number of channels in the input and the number of channels in the 1x1 block are the same. Hence, the output has the same number of channels as the number of 1x1 filters*

Hence, 1x1 convolution is useful when we want to shrink the number of channels or perform any feature transformation. This results in reducing the computational cost. 1x1 is used in a number of Deep Learning architectures like ResNet and Inception. We will now continue our discussion with the Inception network.

7.5.3 GoogLeNet architecture

We discussed the motivation behind creating the GoogLeNet in the last section. The complete GoogLeNet architecture is shown in Figure 7-9. The blocks in blue represent convolution, red are pooling, yellow are softmax, and green are others.

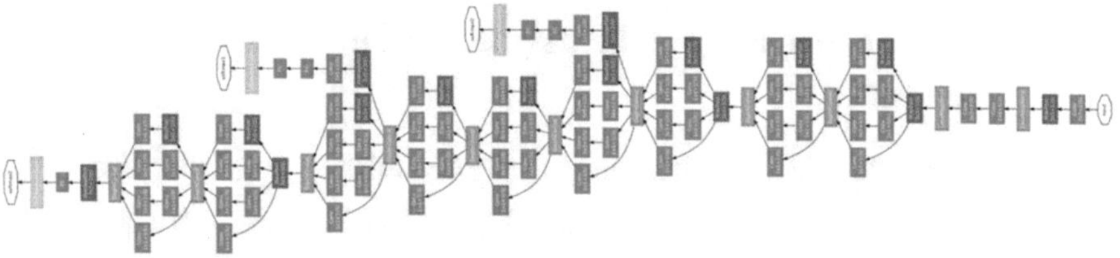

Figure 7-9. *The complete GoogLeNet architecture. Here, blue represents convolution, red blocks are the pooling blocks, while yellow are the softmax ones. We are zooming in on one of the sections later. The image has been taken from* https://arxiv.org/pdf/1409.4842v1.pdf

There are a few important properties about the network:

1. The inception network consists of concatenated blocks of the Inception module.

2. There are nine Inception modules which have been stacked linearly.

3.   There are three softmax branches (in yellow in Figure 7-9) at different positions. Out of these three, two are in the middle part of the network acting as auxiliary classifiers. They ensure that the intermediate features are good for the network to learn and give regularization effects.

4.   The two softmax compute the auxiliary loss. The net loss is the weighted loss of the auxiliary loss and the real loss. The auxiliary loss is useful during the training and not considered for the final classification.

5.   It has 27 layers (22 layers + 5 pooling layers).

6.   There are close to 5 million parameters in the network.

We are now zooming in on one of the cropped versions from the network to examine the network better (Figure 7-10). Note how the softmax classifier (shown in the yellow block) has been added – to address the problem of vanishing gradients and overfitting. The final loss is the weighted loss of the auxiliary loss and the real loss of the network.

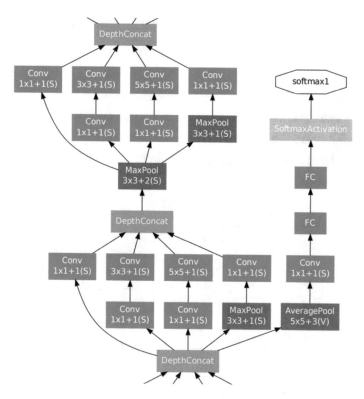

Figure 7-10. *A zoomed-in version of a section from the inception network. Note how the softmax classifier has been added (shown in yellow)*

Inception v1 proved to be a great solution by getting the first place in ILSVRC2014 and having a 6.67% top-5 error rate.

But the researchers did not stop here. They further improved the solution by proposing Inception v2 and Inception v3 which we are discussing next.

7.5.4 Improvements in Inception v2

Inception versions 2 and 3 were discussed in the following paper: https://arxiv.org/pdf/1512.00567v3.pdf. The motivation was to improve the accuracy and reduce the complexity of the model and hence the computation cost.

In Inception v2, there were the following improvements:

1. 5x5 convolutions were factored to two 3x3 convolutions. It was done to improve the computation speed and led to enhanced performance too. It is shown in Figure 7-11. In the figure on the left, we have the original Inception module, and the one on the right is the revised Inception module.

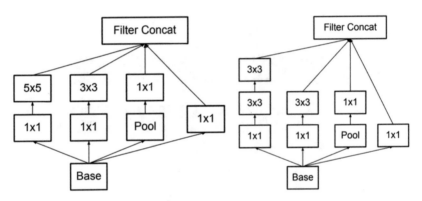

Figure 7-11. *Factorization of 5x5 convolutions to two blocks of 3x3 led to the improvement in the computation speed and the overall accuracy of the solution. The image has been taken from* https://arxiv.org/pdf/1512.00567v3.pdf

2. The second improvement was the convolutions were factorized such that a filter of nxn size is changed to a combination of 1xn and nx1 as shown in Figure 7-12. For example, 5x5 is changed to performing 1x5 first and then 5x1. This further improved the computation efficiency.

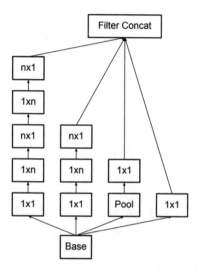

Figure 7-12. *Note how nxn conv can be represented as 1xn and nx1. For example, if we put n=5, then 5x5 is changed as 1x5 and 5x1. The image has been taken from* https://arxiv.org/ pdf/1512.00567v3.pdf

3. With an increase in the depth, the dimensions reduce and hence there can be a loss of information. Hence, an improvement was suggested that the filter banks were made wider instead of going deeper as shown in Figure 7-13.

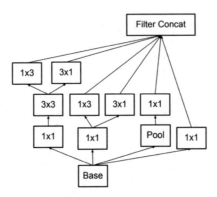

Figure 7-13. *The models are made wider instead of deeper. With an increase in depth, the dimensions are reduced drastically, which is an information loss. The image has been taken from* `https://arxiv.org/pdf/1512.00567v3.pdf`

The researchers quoted:

Although our network is 42 layers deep, our computation cost is only about 2.5 higher than that of GoogLeNet and it is still much more efficient than VGGNet.

Moving ahead, in Inception v3, in addition to the preceding improvements, the significant addition was the use of label smoothing which is a regularizing technique to tackle overfitting. The mathematical proof is beyond the scope of the book. In addition, RMSProp was used as an optimizer, and the auxiliary classifier's fully connected layer is batch normalized. It achieved 3.58% top-5 error on an ensemble of four models which is nearly half of the original GoogLeNet model.

There were further improvements in the form of Inception v4 and Inception-ResNet. It outperformed the previous versions, and an ensemble of 3xInception-ResNet(v2) and 1xInceptionv4 resulted in 3.08% top-5 error.

With this, we have completed the discussion on Inception networks.

Both Inception and ResNet are one of the most widely used networks when it comes to really deep Neural Networks. Using Transfer Learning, they can be used for generating fantastic results and are proving to be a real boon to the computer vision problems.

We will now continue studying the video analytics problems we started at the start of the chapter.

7.6 Video analytics

Video analytics start with processing the videos. As we can see through our eyes and process the contents of a video using our memory and brain, computers can also see – through a camera. And to understand the contents of that video, Deep Learning is providing the necessary support.

Videos are a rich source of information but at the same time are equally complex. In image classification, we take an input image, process it to extract features using CNN, and then classify the image based on the features. In the case of video classification, we first extract the frames from the video and then classify the frames. So, video processing is not one task; rather, it is a collection of subtasks. OpenCV is one of the most popular libraries for video analytics. We are going to use Deep Learning–based solutions for video analytics.

The steps in video classification using Deep Learning are

1. We first get the frames from the video and divide them into training and validation sets.

2. We then train the network on the training data and optimize the accuracy.

3. We will validate on the validation dataset to get the final model.

4. For the unseen new video, we will first grab the frame from the video and then classify the same.

As we can see, the steps are pretty much the same like any image classification solution. The additional step is for the new video – where we first grab a frame and then classify it.

In the next section, we are creating a video classification solution using Inception v3 and ResNet.

7.7 Python solution using ResNet and Inception v3

Now we will create a Python solution for video analytics. For this, we are going to train a network on a Sports dataset and use it to make predictions for a video file.

You can download the dataset from `https://github.com/jurjsorinliviu/Sports-Type-Classifier`. The dataset has images of multiple types of sports. We are going to build a classifier for cricket, hockey, and chess. The dataset and the code is uploaded to the GitHub repo at `https://github.com/Apress/computer-vision-using-deep-learning/tree/main/Chapter7`.

Some examples of images of cricket, hockey, and chess are shown as follows.

Step 1: Load all the required libraries.

```python
import matplotlib

from tensorflow.keras.preprocessing.image import
ImageDataGenerator
from tensorflow.keras.optimizers import SGD
from sklearn.preprocessing import LabelBinarizer
from tensorflow.keras import optimizers
from sklearn.model_selection import train_test_split
```

```
from sklearn.metrics import classification_report
from tensorflow.keras.layers import AveragePooling2D
from tensorflow.keras.applications import InceptionV3
from tensorflow.keras.layers import Dropout
from tensorflow.keras.layers import Flatten
from tensorflow.keras.layers import Dense
from tensorflow.keras.layers import Input
from tensorflow.keras.models import Model
from imutils import paths
import matplotlib.pyplot as plt
import numpy as np
import cv2
import os
```

Step 2: Set the labels for the sports we are interested in.

```
game_labels = set(["cricket", "hockey", "chess"])
```

Step 3: Set the value for other variables like location, path, and so on. We will also initiate two lists – complete_data and complete_label – which will be used for holding the values at a later stage.

```
location = "/Users/vaibhavverdhan/BackupOfOfficeMac/Book/
Restart/Apress/Chapter7/Sports-Type-Classifier-master/data"
data_path = list(paths.list_images(location))
complete_data = []
complete_labels = []
```

Step 4: Load the Sports dataset now and read their corresponding labels. The input size is 299x299 because we are training an Inception v3 first. For ResNet, the size is 224x224.

```
for data in data_path:
    # extract the class label from the filename
    class_label = data.split("/")[-2]
```

```
if class_label not in game_labels:
    #print("Not used class lable",class_label)
    continue
#print("Used class lable",class_label)
image = cv2.imread(data)
image = cv2.cvtColor(image, cv2.COLOR_BGR2RGB)
image = cv2.resize(image, (299, 299))

complete_data.append(image)
complete_labels.append(class_label)
```

Step 5: Convert the labels to numpy arrays.

```
complete_data = np.array(complete_data)
complete_labels = np.array(complete_labels)
```

Step 6: One-hot encoding is done for the labels now.

```
label_binarizer = LabelBinarizer()
complete_labels = label_binarizer.fit_transform(complete_
labels)
```

Step 7: Divide the data into 80% training data and 20% testing data.

```
(x_train, x_test, y_train, y_test) = train_test_split(complete_
data, complete_labels,
    test_size=0.20, stratify=complete_labels, random_state=5)
```

Step 8: We will now initialize the data augmentation object for the training data.

```
training_augumentation = ImageDataGenerator(
    rotation_range=25,
    zoom_range=0.12,
    width_shift_range=0.4,
    height_shift_range=0.4,
```

```
    shear_range=0.10,
    horizontal_flip=True,
    fill_mode="nearest")
```

Step 9: We are now initializing the testing data augmentation object. Next, we are defining the ImageNet mean subtraction value for each of the objects.

```
validation_augumentation = ImageDataGenerator()

mean = np.array([122.6, 115.5, 105.9], dtype="float32")
training_augumentation.mean = mean
validation_augumentation.mean = mean
```

Step 10: Load the Inception network now. This model will serve as the base model.

```
inceptionModel = InceptionV3(weights="imagenet", include_
top=False,
    input_tensor=Input(shape=(299, 299, 3)))
```

Step 11: We will now make the head of the model which will be placed on the top of the base model.

```
outModel = inceptionModel.output
outModel = AveragePooling2D(pool_size=(5, 5))(outModel)
outModel = Flatten(name="flatten")(outModel)
outModel = Dense(512, activation="relu")(outModel)
outModel = Dropout(0.6)(outModel)
outModel = Dense(len(label_binarizer.classes_),
activation="softmax")(outModel)
```

Step 12: We get the final model and make the base model layers as nontrainable.

```
final_model = Model(inputs=inceptionModel.input,
outputs=outModel)
for layer in inceptionModel.layers:
    layer.trainable = False
```

Step 13: We have studied the remaining steps in detail in the last chapters, which are about setting the hyperparameters and fitting the model.

```
num_epochs = 5
learning_rate = 0.1
learning_decay = 1e-6
learning_drop = 20
batch_size = 32
sgd = optimizers.SGD(lr=learning_rate, decay=learning_decay,
momentum=0.9, nesterov=True)
final_model.compile(loss='categorical_crossentropy', optimizer=
sgd,metrics=['accuracy'])
model_fit = final_model.fit(
    x=training_augumentation.flow(x_train, y_train, batch_
    size=batch_size),
    steps_per_epoch=len(x_train) // batch_size,
    validation_data=validation_augumentation.flow(x_test,
    y_test),
    validation_steps=len(x_test) // batch_size,
    epochs=num_epochs)
```

```
Epoch 1/5
11/11 [==============================] - 52s 5s/step - loss: 10.7731 - acc: 0.3333
43/43 [==============================] - 217s 5s/step - loss: 10.7571 - acc: 0.3326 - val_loss: 10.7731 - val_acc: 0.
3333
Epoch 2/5
11/11 [==============================] - 37s 3s/step - loss: 10.6691 - acc: 0.3333
43/43 [==============================] - 208s 5s/step - loss: 10.7571 - acc: 0.3326 - val_loss: 10.6691 - val_acc: 0.
3333
Epoch 3/5
11/11 [==============================] - 37s 3s/step - loss: 10.7940 - acc: 0.3333
43/43 [==============================] - 195s 5s/step - loss: 10.7457 - acc: 0.3326 - val_loss: 10.7940 - val_acc: 0.
3333
Epoch 4/5
11/11 [==============================] - 38s 3s/step - loss: 10.7315 - acc: 0.3333
43/43 [==============================] - 195s 5s/step - loss: 10.7187 - acc: 0.3333 - val_loss: 10.7315 - val_acc: 0.
3333
Epoch 5/5
11/11 [==============================] - 39s 4s/step - loss: 10.7315 - acc: 0.3333
43/43 [==============================] - 201s 5s/step - loss: 10.7189 - acc: 0.3333 - val_loss: 10.7315 - val_acc: 0.
3333
```

Step 14: We get the training/testing accuracy and loss.

```python
import matplotlib.pyplot as plt
f, ax = plt.subplots()
ax.plot([None] + model_fit.history['acc'], 'o-')
ax.plot([None] + model_fit.history['val_acc'], 'x-')
ax.legend(['Train acc', 'Validation acc'], loc = 0)
ax.set_title('Training/Validation acc per Epoch')
ax.set_xlabel('Epoch')
ax.set_ylabel('acc')

import matplotlib.pyplot as plt
f, ax = plt.subplots()
ax.plot([None] + model_fit.history['loss'], 'o-')
ax.plot([None] + model_fit.history['val_loss'], 'x-')
ax.legend(['Train loss', 'Validation loss'], loc = 0)
ax.set_title('Training/Validation loss per Epoch')
ax.set_xlabel('Epoch')
ax.set_ylabel('Loss')

predictions = model_fit.model.predict(testX)
from sklearn.metrics import confusion_matrix
import numpy as np
rounded_labels=np.argmax(testY, axis=1)
rounded_labels[1]
```

```
cm = confusion_matrix(rounded_labels,
np.argmax(predictions,axis=1))
def plot_confusion_matrix(cm):
    cm = [row/sum(row)    for row in cm]
    fig = plt.figure(figsize=(10, 10))
    ax = fig.add_subplot(111)
    cax = ax.matshow(cm, cmap=plt.cm.Oranges)
    fig.colorbar(cax)
    plt.title('Confusion Matrix')
    plt.xlabel('Predicted Class IDs')
    plt.ylabel('True Class IDs')
    plt.show()
plot_confusion_matrix(cm)
```

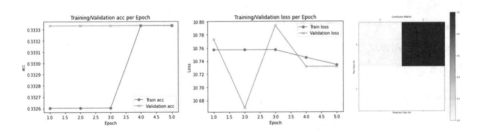

We can analyze that the network is not good enough for predictions.

Step 15: We will now implement ResNet. The input size changes to 224x224, and everything remains the same. We are also changing the sports classes.

```
game_labels = set(["cricket", "swimming", "wrestling"])
```

Step 16: The complete code is at the GitHub link. We are providing the output here.

```
Epoch 1/5
19/19 [==============================] - 48s 3s/step - loss: 7.8011 - acc: 0.3077
86/86 [==============================] - 619s 7s/step - loss: 1.1110 - acc: 0.6122 - val_loss: 7.8011 - val_acc: 0.30
77
Epoch 2/5
19/19 [==============================] - 49s 3s/step - loss: 0.8106 - acc: 0.7316
86/86 [==============================] - 914s 11s/step - loss: 0.6576 - acc: 0.7295 - val_loss: 0.8106 - val_acc: 0.7
316
Epoch 3/5
19/19 [==============================] - 44s 2s/step - loss: 0.7306 - acc: 0.7692
86/86 [==============================] - 601s 7s/step - loss: 0.5137 - acc: 0.7999 - val_loss: 0.7306 - val_acc: 0.76
92
Epoch 4/5
19/19 [==============================] - 44s 2s/step - loss: 0.6629 - acc: 0.7248
86/86 [==============================] - 736s 9s/step - loss: 0.4913 - acc: 0.8087 - val_loss: 0.6629 - val_acc: 0.72
48
Epoch 5/5
19/19 [==============================] - 45s 2s/step - loss: 0.4514 - acc: 0.8581
86/86 [==============================] - 624s 7s/step - loss: 0.4151 - acc: 0.8482 - val_loss: 0.4514 - val_acc: 0.85
81
```

The algorithm is generating a good validation accuracy of 85.81%.

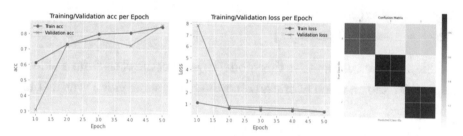

The model is saved, and then we use it for making predictions for a sample image to check if it is able to predict.

```
model_fit.model.save("sport_classification_model.h5")
```

Step 17: We have covered these steps already in the previous chapters.

```
file = open("sport_classification", "wb")
file.write(pickle.dumps(label_binarizer))
file.close()
modelToBeUsed = load_model("sport_classification_model.h5")
labels = pickle.loads(open("sport_classification", "rb").
read())
import numpy as np
from keras.preprocessing import image
an_image =image.load_img('/Users/vaibhavverdhan/
BackupOfOfficeMac/Book/Restart/Apress/Chapter7/Sports-Type-
```

```
Classifier-master/data/cricket/00000000.jpg',target_size
=(224,224))# Load the image
# The image is now getting converted to array of numbers
an_image =image.img_to_array(an_image)
#Let us now expand it's dimensions. It will improve the
prediction power
an_image =np.expand_dims(an_image, axis =0)
# call the predict method here
verdict = modelToBeUsed.predict(an_image)
i = np.argmax(verdict)
label = labels.classes_[i]
```

Step 18: We will now use this model to predict the class from a video of a sport. We took a video of cricket recording. The same video is available at GitHub too.

Step 19: Capture the video in an object.

```
video = cv2.VideoCapture(path_video)
```

Step 20: We are going to iterate over all the frames of the video. For this, we are going to set an indicator isVideoGrabbed as 1 initially. When the end of the video is reached, isVideoGrabbed will become zero, and then we can break from the loop.

We are looping in a while loop. When a frame is grabbed, it is an image and hence is converted to the necessary size and fed to the model for prediction.

```
isVideoGrabbed = 1
while isVideoGrabbed:
    (isVideoGrabbed, video_frame) = video.read()

    if not isVideoGrabbed:
        print("done")
        break
```

```
video_frame = cv2.cvtColor(video_frame, cv2.COLOR_BGR2RGB)
video_frame = cv2.resize(video_frame, (224, 224)).
astype("float32")
video_frame -= mean
prediction_game = modelToBeUsed.predict(np.expand_
dims(video_frame, axis=0))[0]
i = np.argmax(verdict)
game = labels.classes_[i]
#print(game)
```

Step 21: We can hence generate the predictions for the entire video frame by frame. This way, we can use Neural Networks to have a look at a video and predict the sports being played in it.

Note   There can be some ambiguities in the predictions sometimes. We can improve the final predictions by taking a mode of all the predictions made for the frames.

This concludes our Python solution using ResNet and Inception v3 network. As we can observe, using transfer learning, it is not a big challenge to harness the powers of these very deep Neural Networks. But creating a tuned solution is still a tough job. In the preceding example, we can analyze the difference between the respective accuracies of ResNet and Inception v3 network. It depends on the dataset and the number of images available.

With this, we have completed the implementation of Python solution. We can now progress to the summary section.

7.8 Summary

Videos are continuous frames of images and a great source of entertainment. With the improvements in the technology space, smaller and lighter cameras, integration of cameras in smartphones, and penetration of social media, a humongous number of videos are being created. The Deep Learning architectures offer a great deal of flexibility to analyze them and generate insights. But video analytics is still less explored as compared to images. Videos are a combination of sound and images. There is still a lot of scope in this space. Deep Learning architectures are pushing the boundaries.

Deep Learning architectures are increasingly becoming deeper. And there is a misconception that the deeper the network is, the better is the performance. With an increase in depth, the complexity level increases. The dimensions reduce which is a loss of information. The network might start to overfit. Hence, novel and innovative solutions are needed of the hour. Sometimes, a different thought provides a more robust solution.

This chapter examines two important networks – ResNet and Inception. Both of these networks are quite innovative and enhance the capabilities. We studied the structure and the innovative nature of these networks. The networks are widely used due to their great performance.

In this chapter, we also studied concepts of video analytics and video processing. We created a Python solution using ResNet and Inception v3 network. Transfer learning was used by using pre-trained weights.

In the next chapter, which is the last chapter of the book, we are discussing the entire process of developing a Deep Learning solution. It also examines the issues we face, solutions for them, and the best practices followed. Quite an important one!

You can now proceed to the exercise section.

REVIEW EXERCISES

Q1. What is the purpose of skip connections and how are they useful?

Q2. What is the problem of vanishing gradients and how can we rectify it?

Q3. What is the improvement between Inception v1 and Inception v3 networks?

Q4. Use VGG and AlexNet for the Sports classification problem we solved in the chapter and compare the performance between networks.

Q5. Get the video dataset from `www.tensorflow.org/datasets/ catalog/ucf101`. The dataset has 101 distinct classes; use it to perform classifications.

Q6. Get the INO sensor dataset from `www.ino.ca/en/technologies/ video-analytics-dataset/`. It has simultaneous color and thermal images. Develop classification algorithms using ResNet.

7.8.1 Further readings

1. Explore the papers at the following links:

   a. "Densely Connected Convolutional Networks": `https://ieeexplore.ieee.org/document/8099726`

   b. "Very Deep Convolutional Networks for Large-Scale Image Recognition": `https://arxiv.org/ abs/1409.1556`

   c. "Identity Mappings in Deep Residual Networks": `https://arxiv.org/abs/1603.05027`

   d. "Dropout: A Simple Way to Prevent Neural Networks from Overfitting": `https://jmlr.org/papers/ volume15/srivastava14a/srivastava14a.pdf`

CHAPTER 8

End-to-End Model Development

Sometimes it is the journey that teaches you a lot about your destination.

—Drake

Deep Learning is a long and tedious journey. It requires practice and continuous rigor. The path to success requires meticulous planning, dedication, constant practice, and patience. In this journey, you have already taken the very first steps.

We started this book with the core concepts of computer vision. We developed solutions using OpenCV. And then we explored concepts of convolutional Neural Networks – various layers, functions, and respective outputs.

In this book so far, we have discussed multiple network architectures. In the process, we discussed their respective components, technical details, pros and cons, and successive improvement. We have also solved use cases of binary image classification, multiclass image classification, object detection, face detection and recognition, and video analytics. In this final chapter of the book, we will explore the end-to-end model development cycle including deployment, best practices, common pitfalls, and challenges faced. We will also deep dive into the requirements for the

© Vaibhav Verdhan 2021
V. Verdhan, *Computer Vision Using Deep Learning*,
https://doi.org/10.1007/978-1-4842-6616-8_8

project and examine concepts of transfer learning into more detail. We will compare and benchmark the performance of various architectures. And finally, we will discuss the next steps for you.

In this last chapter of the book, we are going to cover these topics:

1. Deep Learning project requirements

2. End-to-end model development process

3. Image augmentation

4. Common mistakes and best practices

5. Model deployment and maintenance

Welcome to the eighth and last chapter and all the very best!

8.1 Technical requirements

The code and datasets for the chapter are uploaded at the GitHub link `https://github.com/Apress/computer-vision-using-deep-learning/ tree/main/Chapter8` for this book. For this chapter, a GPU is good enough to execute the code, and you can use Google Colaboratory. We will be using Python Jupyter Notebook.

Let's proceed with requirements in a Deep Learning project.

8.2 Deep Learning project requirements

Like any other project, Deep Learning–based projects are also meant to have all the components for a successful project. We are describing the components for a project working on an image, which are shown in Figure 8-1.

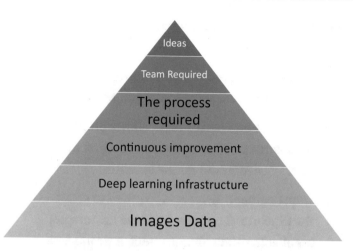

Figure 8-1. *Deep Learning computer vision projects require the following components for development and execution. It is similar to any other project process*

The salient components for a successful Deep Learning project are

1. Ideation or ideas refer to a constant brainstorming which is required for Deep Learning projects to be successful. The ideation process ensures a robust line of ideas and solutions in case of issues faced during the project. A good mix of business knowledge and deep learning/machine learning expertise is required. There are other roles required along with the two mentioned which is the next point – team structure.

2. The team needed for a machine learning project requires a mix of business subject matter experts, professionals with technical acumen, data engineering team, software engineering team, project managers, and IT team.

    a. Subject matter experts ensure that the project is on the right path to success in achieving the business goal.

b. Data science team is responsible for developing the algorithm.

c. Project managers or scrum masters run the show and manage the entire project.

d. Software engineering team allows proper deployment of the model and creation of interfaces required for the solution.

e. Data engineering team is required to create the pipeline to transfer and save the images; for effective data management, a strong data engineering team is required.

f. IT team ensures a proper infrastructure is in place for the entire interface and the solution.

3. A robust and concrete process ensures that no step is being ignored and we are setting the project for success. The process of Deep Learning projects is being discussed in detail in the next section.

4. Continuous improvement is a product of feedback and monitoring. Once the algorithm has been deployed in the production system, we should constantly monitor the performance and improve the capabilities through a feedback mechanism. Monitoring also ensures that in case the solution falls below the required threshold of accuracy, the solution is checked and improved. We will study more on model maintenance in subsequent sections.

5. Deep Learning infrastructure is the backbone for the project. Without access to good machines, processors, GPU, storage, and so on, it becomes

really tough and sometimes impossible to train a robust Deep Learning–based solution. In our standard laptops and desktops with 4GB or 8GB of RAM and standard processors, it is not possible to train a computer vision model using a Neural Network and training on 50,000 images. Hence, a robust infrastructure is needed for the hour. Cloud services like Azure or Google Cloud or Amazon Web Services provide virtual machines which can be used for this purpose, but of course with a cost. We are suggesting a robust hardware required for Deep Learning projects in subsequent sections.

Note   Thanks to Google, we can use Google Colab for free. But Google Colab is not a permanent solution and should not be used for sensitive datasets. Moreover, being a free version, it does not ensure that we do have access to all the power of machines. The Google Colab setup is provided in the Reference.

6.   Datasets are the raw materials which are required to train the algorithm, measure the performance, and monitor the progress in the future. An effective data management is required to ensure that all the images are captured and saved carefully, the training data is effectively used and stored for audit purpose, and unseen and new datasets on which the prediction is made are stored for future reference. A concrete data management process is required to ensure that the project is set for success. We are going to examine this step again in the next section.

A Deep Learning project is a very interesting amalgamation of different teams and skill sets. The algorithm is the heart of the solution, but the algorithm also requires a thorough testing and deployment. The subject matter expert (SME) ensures that the algorithm is able to do justice to the business problem at hand. In a nutshell, a perfect team is required for the solution to work effectively in the real world.

We are now going to study the entire project process in detail, which is the next section.

8.3 Deep Learning project process

Like any other project, Deep Learning–based projects are also meant to solve a business problem. And like any other project, they need to be deployed into production. In this section, we will discuss the salient steps in the process of a Deep Learning project.

The very first step in the Deep Learning project is defining the business problem. The entire process is shown by means of a diagram in Figure 8-2.

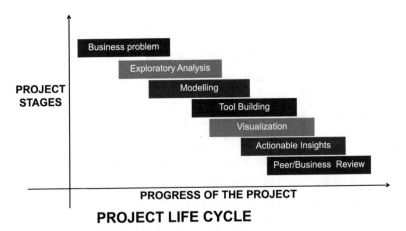

Figure 8-2. *Various stages in a Deep Learning project. It starts with defining a robust business problem, followed by working with data and modeling and maintenance*

We are going to discuss through each of the steps in the model building process. We are first going to explore the business problem definition in the next section.

8.4 Business problem definition

Business problem definition is the core requirement of the project. Often, the business problem is not clearly defined and not scoped properly. There are scope creeps throughout the project duration and lags and delays. Sometimes, it is observed that the expected output and the actual results do not meet, which creates friction between teams, and in many cases the entire project has to be scrapped.

Common challenges faced while defining business problems are

1. Business problems which are vague and ill-defined are a nuisance. For example, "we have to increase the revenue." This business problem has no logical sense and can be reframed.

2. Sometimes, the business objectives are very ambitious. For example, "we have to reduce the cost by 80% in the next 1 week." It might not be feasible to achieve the objective in the said time frame. Such problems have to be improved.

3. It has been observed that many times there is a lack of a proper KPI (key performance indicator) associated with the business problem. For example, "we have to increase the revenue" is a very broad statement. Without any measurable metric, it is very difficult to gauge the performance of the solution.

Hence, defining a good business problem is of paramount importance. We are defining a few components of a good business problem:

1. Clear and concise: A good business problem focuses on the objective in target. For example, "The business wishes to automate the attendance system of the organization. And for this purpose, an automatic face identification system needs to be created." This problem still has more components, but the business problem is clearly defined here.

2. Measurable: A business problem can be measured using a KPI. Without this measurement criterion, it will be difficult to gauge the actual performance of the system and what the errors are in the solution. To improve the performance of the system, there has to be a KPI which has to be optimized to achieve the best results. For example, in the preceding example, we can extend the problem as "The business wishes to automate the attendance system of the organization. And for this purpose, an automatic face identification system needs to be created. The expected accuracy of the system is 95% with a false accept rate of less than 0.01%."

3. Achievable: A good business problem is achievable and pragmatically possible. It should be practical enough to conceptualize and implement. For example, in the preceding example of face detection, it will not be a good idea to expect 100% accuracy with 0% false accept rates. However, there are some domains like medical imaging for cancer detection where a very high rate of accuracy is desired, but achieving a perfect score of 100% accuracy might not be achievable.

4.   Maintainable: A forward-looking business problem plans about the future state of the solution. The monitoring of the results, maintenance of the algorithm, refresh cycle, and next steps are a part of the larger scope of the business problem.

Having a well-defined business problem results in a well-managed development process and a fruitful solution at the end. At the same time, it is imperative that the business stakeholders are made a part of the discussions and processes. They can course correct the solution by imparting the SME (subject matter expert) knowledge.

Let us examine the business problem definition by means of two examples in the computer vision domain.

8.4.1 Face detection for surveillance

Consider we have a retail store. The business problem can be identified as described in the following discussion.

"There is a need to improve the security systems in the less monitored areas of the store. The retailer needs to constantly monitor the areas and detect the shoplifting or any antisocial behavior in the store. The current process of surveillance is mostly manual. At the same time, it is also required to detect and match the faces of the customers with the database of people barred from entering the store, so that the store can take appropriate measures."

In such a business use case, the business objective is to

1.   Constantly monitor the areas in the less monitored spaces in the store

2.   Detect any unsocial activity within the store area

3.   Detect and identify the people who are not allowed inside the store by the store authorities

To complete the problem statement further, the KPI around the accuracy of detection and the false accept/reject rates should be decided. In the preceding business problem:

- True positive: Correctly classifying the person in the store as "acceptable" who are allowed inside the store.

- True negative: Correctly classifying the person in the store as "not acceptable" who are not allowed inside the store.

- False positive: Incorrectly classifying the person in the store as "acceptable" who should not be allowed in the store.

- False negative: Incorrectly classifying the person in the store as "not acceptable" who should be allowed in the store.

Hence, in the preceding business case, depending on the KPI, we will optimize the solution.

We will now discuss the second business use case for computer vision using Deep Learning.

8.4.1.1 Defect detection for manufacturing

Consider we have a mobile phone manufacturing unit. It manufactures mobile phones on different manufacturing lines. During the process of manufacturing, it is a possibility that a foreign particle might get introduced in the mobile chamber – foreign particles like strings, hair, plastic pieces, debris, and so on. The size can be very small like 200 microns, 300 microns, and so on. The business problem can be identified as described in the following discussion.

"The manufacturing plant wishes to detect the presence of any foreign material inside the mobile chambers. The need is to detect all types of foreign matter like strings, hair, plastic pieces, debris which can be of varied sizes and at various locations. A camera has been placed on top of the manufacturing lines which is clicking the images of each incoming product. In real time, a Deep Learning–based network is going to detect the presence of foreign particles and is going to accept or reject the product."

In such a business use case, the business objective is to

1. Constantly monitor the images of the product manufactured in real time

2. Detect the presence of any foreign particle within the product

To complete the problem statement further, the KPI around the accuracy of detection and the false accept/reject rates should be decided. In the preceding business problem:

- True positive: Correctly classifying the product as good which does not contain any foreign matter

- True negative: Correctly classifying the product as bad which contains the foreign matter

- False positive: Incorrectly accepting the product which contains the foreign matter

- False negative: Incorrectly rejecting the product which does not contain the foreign matter

Hence, in the preceding business case, depending on the KPI, we will optimize the solution.

Once the business problem definition is finalized, we move to the next steps of exploratory data analysis, model building, and so on (Figure 8-2). We are describing the steps in more detail in Figure 8-3.

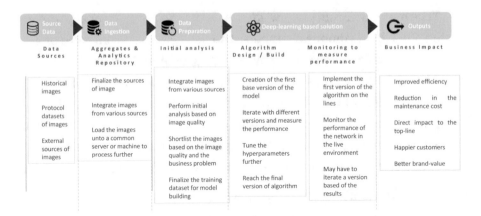

Figure 8-3. *Detailed steps in a Deep Learning modeling process. At each step, we work on various attributes of images and create a robust network. It requires a great deal of teamwork and expertise to deliver the project*

The business problem definition sets the goal for us. It means we are ready to work with the datasets and then proceed to training. The next step is the data discovery phase which we are discussing next.

8.4.2 Source data or data discovery phase

Once we have completed the first step around freezing the business problem, scoping it, and defining the KPIs and performance measurement parameters, we then proceed to the data discovery phase.

In this phase, primarily, we scout for the data, or in the case of computer vision, we look for images. Let us understand by means of the same example cases we discussed in the business problem definition step.

8.4.2.1 Face detection for identification

The business problem is "to identify the face shown to the camera, and if it is matched with the database of employees, mark the attendance as present."

In such a use case, the raw data is going to be the images of the employee's face. The images have to be from different angles and as clear as possible. If we ask the employees to get the pictures clicked themselves and share with the team, there is a danger of aspect ratio, dimensions, background lighting, brightness, and so on. Moreover, different employees will use different modes to click pictures, and hence the raw data generated can be quite different. Hence, in such a case, it is advisable to get every image captured in a similar environment to maintain consistency. Preferably, a camera can be set wherein each employee can come and get their pictures clicked.

But such an arrangement is not a requirement for the network to be trained. The network can be trained on different sizes and types of faces. The advantage with the suggested method can be improved accuracy and computational advantage while training the algorithm. The network can be trained without such an arrangement.

In this use case, we will capture the raw images of faces to train the network. We have already studied the various face detection networks in Chapter 6. These training images have to be saved for future reference purpose and for audit trail. We have already discussed in detail the training data management process in the data management process in the last section. We will discuss the attributes of optimized training data in subsequent sections.

We now move to the next case of live monitoring on a manufacturing line.

8.4.2.2 Live environment on a manufacturing line

The business problem is "to analyze the images manufactured in the mobile phone manufacturing plant in the live environment and assess if there is a foreign particle present in the product."

For this business use case, we will search for historical data to train the network. The training data will be composed of good examples of products having no foreign matter and bad examples which have a foreign particle present inside them. The image dataset has to be complete and can include many historical images. It is a possibility that we do not get a huge number of bad images; hence, those images might need to be created manually. It is suggested that we can have a camera to click the images which will provide the raw images. But these raw images would have to be graded manually into good and bad classes so that they can be fed to the network for training.

The images have to be representative enough and should contain all the possible variations. We will discuss more on the image quality in the next section and will also examine the attributes of an optimized training data.

We now move to the next phase, which is data ingestion or data management.

8.5 Data ingestion or data management

Data management is required to ensure that we have an effective platform to save our images and use them to train the algorithm. It also ensures that all the monitoring datasets are saved for future references. The new and unseen datasets on which the algorithm makes the predictions are required for future improvements.

A proper data management platform has the following attributes:

1. During the data discovery phase, we have finalized all the data sources we wish to use. During the data management phase, we first finalize all the sources we have shortlisted in the last phase.

2. All the image sources are then integrated to ensure
    that we have all the artifacts at the same platform.
    The data sources can be offline and online and can
    be curated and sometimes manually created. The
    images are saved and analyzed over a period of
    time and from multiple sources. It will also include
    getting the images which are fresh and most recent.

    a. For the face detection problem, the dataset
        includes historical face datasets which have
        been captured over the last few months. For the
        manufacturing line defect detection system,
        it can be a historical dataset from multiple
        manufacturing lines and months.

    b. For face detection, it might include the images
        captured recently, and for manufacturing
        detection problem, it will include the live images
        being captured in the live environment.

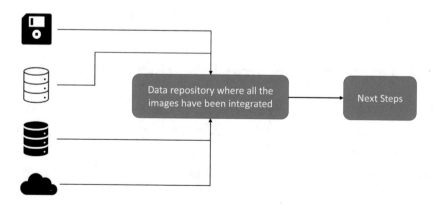

Figure 8-4. *Data repository where all the images from multiple*
sources can be integrated for further usage

3. All the data points are then loaded to a repository
    (Figure 8-4). This repository will be accessed by the
    algorithm to train the network. The repository can
    be a stand-alone server hosted on-premise or can be
    a cloud-based solution using Azure, Google Cloud,
    AWS, and so on. This repository ideally should be
    scalable and can be expanded to save more images,
    as and when required.

4. Data management requires strong data engineering
    skills and involvement of the IT team. The data
    engineering team sets the pipeline for the transfer of
    the images from live environment to the repository,
    allows to save the historical images in the same
    repository, and ensures that the system is regularly
    monitored and stays intact.

Once the data management is in place, we have the images which can
be used for analysis. Now the next step is to analyze the available artifacts
and create the final training dataset which can be used for training the
algorithm, which is the next step we are going to discuss.

8.6 Data preparation and augmentation

Once we have the data ready and stored at a common platform, we start
the initial analysis of the data. We look at the image parameters of sizes,
aspect ratios, and so on. As compared to structured datasets, for images a
lot of EDA (exploratory data analysis) is not possible. But still, we carry out
a sanity check on the image quality.

For the images we have saved and loaded at the server, we analyze
the different types of classes we have to classify vis-à-vis the number of
examples available for each of the classes.

Note   The cliché of "garbage in, garbage out" holds true. If the training dataset is biased, the results are not going to be concrete.

To have a robust model, we need to have a representative dataset which is complete, concrete, and not biased. A few of the attributes of a good training dataset are

1. The dataset should cover the participation from each of the interfaces which are going to use the solution. For example, in the case of manufacturing defects discussed earlier, if ten manufacturing lines are going to use them, we should have data from all the ten lines to ensure representation. Else, it is a possibility that the solution is working well on most of the lines but not on those lines which do not have enough representation in the training dataset.

2. The dataset should have enough examples of good and bad images. In an ideal scenario, we would have an equal representation, but in real world we might not get enough examples. So it is imperative that we concentrate our energies in collecting a robust and representative dataset.

Note   Though there is no perfectly recommended ratio for good and bad training dataset, to avoid bias each class should have at least 10% representation in the final training dataset.

3. If there is an element of time-based dependency, the training dataset should have enough examples adhering to the time factors. For example, in the manufacturing defect problem, we might want to include data from different shifts and different days of the week to the training data.

4. The quality of the images plays a vital role in the final accuracy of the model. We ensure that we include images which are clear and not blurred or hazy. Quite a few times, we do not have a large dataset, and we need to augment the images further which we are discussing in the section next.

5. The output of this step should be the configured training dataset which we wish to use for training the algorithm.

Image augmentation is a crucial step which allows us to ensure we have enough training examples for training the algorithm, which we are discussing now.

8.6.1 Image augmentation

Once we have collected the images, many times we do not have big enough dataset to train the algorithm. It also allows us to add the generalization ability to the network and prevent it from overfitting. For Neural Networks, we require more and more data, and image augmentation can help in artificially increasing the training dataset by creating versions of images. It enhances the ability of the models as the augmented images provide different variations along with the original training dataset.

We can transform the data or in other words manipulate the images using zoom, shift, flip, rotation, mirror-imaging, cropping, and various other methods.

But we have to be cautious too, since we should perform only the variations which we can expect in the real world. For example, if we wish to create a face detection system, it is highly unlikely that we get faces at 180-degree angles, and hence we can avoid such rotations. So based on the business problem at hand, we should choose the augmentation technique.

The Keras Deep Learning library provides a robust mechanism to augment the dataset. There is an ImageDataGenerator which can be used for the purpose of data augmentation. We are creating the solution now.

We are going to use the photo in Figure 8-5 for augmentation purposes.

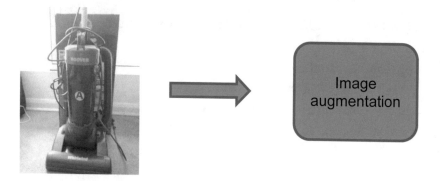

Figure 8-5. *We are going to work on the image of this vacuum cleaner for augmentation purposes*

Step 1: Import all the libraries first.

```
from numpy import expand_dims
from keras.preprocessing.image import load_img
from keras.preprocessing.image import img_to_array
from keras.preprocessing.image import ImageDataGenerator
from matplotlib import pyplot
```

Step 2: Load the image now.

```
sample_image = load_img('Hoover.jpg')
```

Step 3: Convert the image to a numpy array and expand dimensions to one sample.

```
imageData = img_to_array(sample_image)
samples = expand_dims(imageData, 0)
```

Step 4: Create the image data generator now. Here, we are working on the width shift property.

```
dataGenerator = ImageDataGenerator(width_shift_range=[-150,150])
```

Step 5: Prepare the iterator and then generate the plots.

```
dataIterator = dataGenerator.flow(samples, batch_size=1)
for i in range(9):
    pyplot.subplot(250 + 1 + i)
    batch = dataIterator.next()
    image = batch[0].astype('uint8')
    pyplot.imshow(image)
pyplot.show()
```

The output is

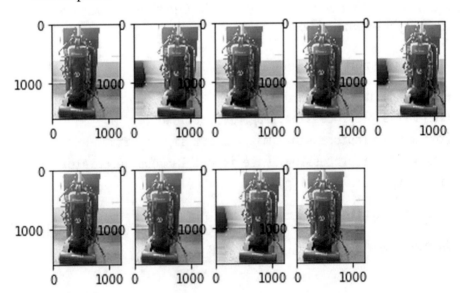

We are using different image generators and get different results. In the next augmentation, we are working on a height shift.

```
dataGenerator = ImageDataGenerator(height_shift_range=[-0.4])
```

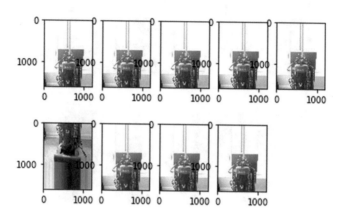

Next, we are zooming the image at different levels.

```
dataGenerator = ImageDataGenerator(zoom_range=[0.15,0.9])
```

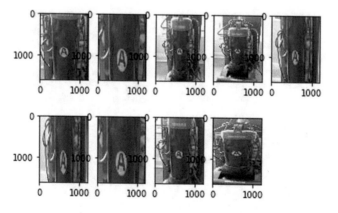

The images are rotated now.

```
dataGenerator = ImageDataGenerator(rotation_range=60)
```

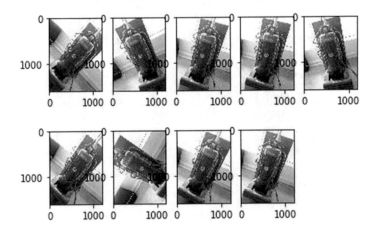

The images are augmented using different values of brightness.

```
dataGenerator = ImageDataGenerator(brightness_range=[0.15,0.9])
```

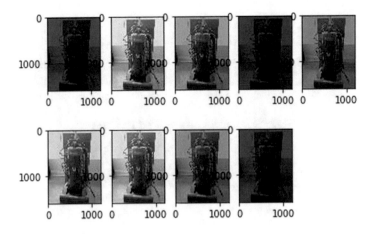

```
dataGenerator = ImageDataGenerator(horizontal_flip=True)
```

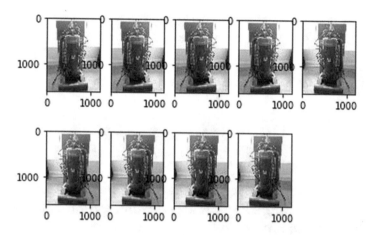

In the preceding examples, we have used different versions of the same image. We need not create these versions separately and save in our database. Saving in a database will result in a huge investment of storage space. Hence, while we are training the network itself, these augmentations can be done within the network itself.

To summarize, image augmentation helps us in expanding the training dataset and enhances the performance of the model. We can shift, flip, crop, and zoom the images to create more versions of the original training images.

Once we have completed configuring the training dataset, the next step will be starting with the modeling of the data, which we are discussing now.

8.7 Deep Learning modeling process

We now can start with modeling. We will take the example of defect detection on the manufacturing lines as the sample use case. We are well aware of the process of training and testing the algorithm. The salient steps are described in the following text and are shown in Figure 8-6.

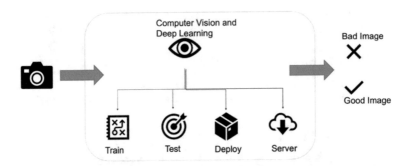

Figure 8-6. *Training, testing, and deploying the model are integral parts of Deep Learning solutions. It generally requires a server setup to put the model in production*

As we can observe, the first step is to train the algorithm on the dataset we have created. The raw data in the first step is divided into training and testing in the ratio of 80:20 or 70:30. Training data is used to train the algorithm, while testing one acts as an unseen dataset and is used to check the performance of the model on the unseen dataset. Most of the time, we iterate and create more than one version of the algorithm. We pick and choose the best model based on performance on the testing data.

Some schools of thought also suggest using train, test, and validation partitions as 60:20:20 ratio. Here, the training dataset is used to train the algorithm, and testing data is used to check the performance on unseen datasets. We will use testing data to check the performance and choose the best algorithm. The validation data, however, will be used only once we have chosen the best algorithm.

We are now all set to start training the network. Generally, we start with testing two or three networks. We can start, for example, with VGG16, Inception v3, and ResNet to train three algorithms. We can use Transfer Learning for it. We have already discussed Transfer Learning in Chapter 5 and used it across the previous chapters. In this section, we are going to examine more on Transfer Learning.

This base version sets the base accuracy, recall, precision, and AUC parameters for us. Then we analyze the misclassifications done by the algorithms. We might have to increase the training dataset and try to improve the base version by tuning the hyperparameters. Ideally, after tuning the model, the performance should improve. We will discuss more on it in this section.

We compare the accuracies, precision, and recall for the networks on training and testing datasets. And then we choose the best network for us. The choice of the network depends on the business problem at hand. Some business problems might want a very high recall, for example, if we wish to detect cancer using image analysis of the body, we would want a near perfect recall rate. In other words, we would want our analysis to detect all the infected patients, even if the precision is low.

So in this step, we primarily focus on the following:

1. We create the first and base version of the model.

2. We iterate with different versions and measures of performance.

3. We tune the hyperparameters to improve the performance.

4. We pick and choose the final solution.

Once the final version of the network is chosen, we test the solution on unseen datasets. Generally, it is done on real-world images to gauge the performance of the model.

We will now discuss some of the important points we should take care of while working on a Deep Learning project. We are starting with Transfer Learning.

8.7.1 Transfer learning

Recall from Chapter 5, where we discussed transfer learning, shown in Figure 8-7. Transfer learning is the process where we use a pre-trained network for our purpose. The researchers use very high computation power and millions of images and train complex networks. We can use those networks to fit our business problems.

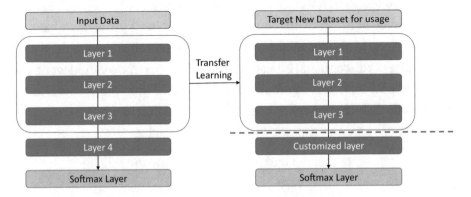

Figure 8-7. *Transfer learning allows us to use pre-trained networks, and we can customize them as per our needs*

In transfer learning, we mentioned that we would want to use pre-trained networks, customize them for our business problem, and train the network. We use the weights and architectures of the base network and modify them to fit our purpose.

There are a few points which are important to note:

1. One has to be really cautious while using pre-trained networks. The choice of the network is important since it plays the central role in the final accuracy. For example, if we have chosen a network trained on text data, it might not give good results for images.

2.   We can use a lower learning rate while trying to use
     a pre-trained model, while generally we would keep
     the weights and the architecture the same.

3.   The initial layers are mostly used for feature extraction
     from the images for the current business problem. Some
     of the layers are used for training, while the rest of them
     can be frozen. In most of the cases, we feed in our images
     and change the final layers while retaining the weights
     and architecture of the network.

4.   Figure 8-8 gives us the directions to pick and choose
     our strategy based on the dataset available to us and
     the similarity of images.

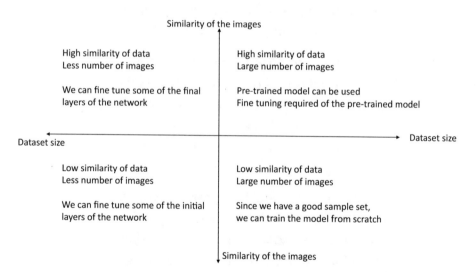

Figure 8-8. *We can customize our strategy as per the dataset size and
similarity of the images with the pre-trained network's images*

As we can observe, our modeling strategy changes as per the dataset.
We iterate with the versions, tune the hyperparameters, and come up with
the best version of the algorithm.

8.7.2 Common mistakes/challenges and boosting performance

The most common challenges we face and the mistakes we make while training the Deep Learning algorithm are:

1. **Data quality**: If the input dataset is noisy, the training will not be fruitful. We also need to ensure that the images are of good quality and not blurred, hazy, cut, very dark, or very white.

2. **Data quantity**: We should ensure that we have enough representations from all the respective classes. Generally, at least 1000 images are suggested for each class, but researchers have trained networks with lesser numbers too.

3. **Training data composition**: The composition of the training data refers to the distribution of the various classes. In the case of binary classification, it refers to the ratio of good vs. bad images. It is vital that each class has at least 10% representation in the final training dataset.

4. **Training dataset** should be representative and complete enough to solve the business problem. In other words, there should be a relationship between the input dataset and the output we wish to receive.

5. **Logs monitoring**: It is a debugging practice which can be used in case we are stuck. We use the print command and get the outputs printed so that we can perform step-by-step debugging of the code.

6. **Augmentation** of the images should be used with caution. Image augmentation is a popular technique to increase the data size, but it does have a regularization effect on the model.

7. **Dataset** should be **shuffled** and should not be in a particular order, else it can lead to bias in the final model.

8. If we are using a pre-trained model, and in case any **preprocessing** is required, it must be computed for the training dataset and then applied to the validation dataset. Also, preprocessing should be the same as required by the original algorithm.

9. **Batch size** used during training can impact the performance. If the batch size is really big, the model might not be able to generalize well.

10. **Weight initialization** is another parameter which plays a vital role. We should try different initializations and monitor the difference.

11. **Overfitting** is a nuisance wherein the testing accuracy is low while the training accuracy is high. It means that the algorithm will not perform well on an unseen dataset. We can use dropout, batch normalization, L1/L2 regularization, and so on to tackle the problem of overfitting.

12. **Underfitting** of the model is an equal challenge we face. To combat underfitting, we can increase the data size, try to increase the complexity by training a deeper network or more number of hidden neurons, or can try a more complex pre-trained network. Reducing regularization might be helpful too.

13. **Visualization** of the training/testing process, accuracy, and loss allows us to visualize the entire end-to-end process. We can monitor the activations, weights, and updates made to the model.

14. We do encounter the problem of **vanishing gradients** while training the network. We have discussed them in Chapter 7. Vanishing gradient problem is the phenomenon when the initial layers of the network cease to learn as the gradient becomes close to zero. There are a few ways to resolve this like ReLU, alternate weight initializations, and variation on gradient descent.

    On the other hand, exploding gradient is an issue in which error gradients can accumulate during the update and can result in very large gradients. It results in an unstable network, and the network is not able to learn anything. Sometimes, we might get NaN (not a number) weight values. We can resolve exploding gradient problems by redesigning the network. Smaller batch size while training can also help. Finally, checking the size of gradients can be helpful in resolving the issue.

15. Sometimes, we encounter **NaN** (not a number) in the results. There are a few reasons and solutions:

    a. NaN can occur if we are dividing by zero.

    b. NaN can occur if the log of a zero or a negative number is being referred.

    c. Generally, we can deal with NaN by changing the learning rate.

    d. If nothing works, we print the logs and analyze the respective outputs layer by layer.

16. Training time might be too high sometimes. During the training process, the weights of each layer change and the activations also change. And hence the overall distribution also changes. It results in high training time. If the dataset is too big, the network is very complex, or the hardware is not very strong, we might have a high training time.

To tackle training time, we can try the following options:

a) Reduce the complexity of the network, but this has to be done with caution as there should not be much impact on the performance of the model.

b) Sometimes, normalization of the data can help in reducing the training time.

c) Iterating with batch size to choose an optimal value for the best training time can also help.

d) Overall, a faster and better hardware will be of much help to reduce the training time of the network.

17. Learning rate impacts the convergence of the model. A high learning rate can lead to low accuracy but will be faster to converge. On the other hand, a very low learning rate will be slower, but the solution will be better. We can observe that in Figure 8-9. Generally, we change the learning rate by a factor of 0.1.

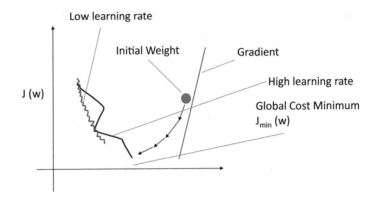

Figure 8-9. *Low learning rate will make the convergence slow, while a high learning rate might not give best results*

18. Sometimes, we disable gradient updates for a few
layers or freeze the wrong layers. A more common
case is we have written any custom layers, and we
have made erroneous computations.

We are giving very simple steps to train a Deep Learning model now:

1. We first create a base version of the solution. For
example, VGG16 and using standard loss functions,
learning rates, and so on.

2. We verify the following points before training:

a. The input data is correct.

b. If preprocessing has to be done, it should match
as required by the original model.

3. In this base version, we use a very small sample size,
maybe 50 images. It ensures that the code syntax is
correct and the model is training. We might get very
low accuracy or the model might overfit, but this
step is generally done.

4. Once this base version is trained, we then add the complete dataset.

5. Once the base version is trained, we add more pieces like data augmentation, regularization, and so on. We tune the hyperparameters and improve the model's performance gradually.

6. And then we proceed to more complex models like ResNet or Inception v3.

Congratulations! Your model is now ready after training and is ready for deployment which is the next step.

8.8 Model deployment and maintenance

We now have the final version of the algorithm with us, which we wish to deploy in a production environment. It simply means that the network will be used to make the predictions in the real world and on fresh unseen images.

There are four important factors which we should consider before choosing and devising a strategy to deploy the model in production:

1. Is the model going to be used in a real-time scenario or in batch mode? If it is a real-time prediction, it is advisable to use API-based deployment.

2. If the model is real time, what is the load of incoming data we are expecting?

3. How much preprocessing is required for the incoming and unseen dataset, and do we expect the incoming format to be drastically different from the format of the training dataset?

4. What is the refresh cycle of the model? If the model is to be refreshed frequently, it is advisable to use the model in offline mode, to minimize software interfaces.

The major techniques to perform deployment are given as follows. There are other solutions too which can be used:

1. One can argue why we can't write the Deep Learning algorithms in the language of the applications. For example, JavaScript might not support these advanced networks which we have discussed in the book. Moreover, it will take a huge amount of time and energy to perform the same task in such languages and will be like "reinventing the wheel."

2. If the core application is in Python, then deployment becomes an easier task. It is an ideal situation as there can be less challenges faced. But still it will require loading the libraries and packages, ensuring all the dependencies are installed and configurations are done.

3. We can configure a Web API and call it to make the predictions for us. The Web API made it easier for cross-language applications to communicate with each other. Hence, if the front end of the application requires results from the Deep Learning model, it just needs to get the URL endpoint from where the API is being served. The front-end application needs to provide the input in a predefined format, and the model can provide the result back. We are discussing major methods to work with API and deploy the Deep Learning model:

    a.   REST API can be created with Flask or Django. Flask is an access point for models and allows us to utilize the model abilities through HTTP requests.

    b.   Docker is becoming the most sought-after choice to deploy the Deep Learning–based models. The model including all of its dependencies can be containerized and packaged at one place. And it allows the server to scale up automatically as per the need. Kubernetes is one of the most famous ways to deploy the machine learning model.

4.   We can also use services like Azure, AWS, and so on to deploy our model. These services not only allow us to train the network but also support in the final deployment.

5.   TensorFlow Serving is also one of the options available to us. It is a high-performance deployment system preferred by Google.

The deployment of the model is the most crucial step. It is the final destination where we would wish our Deep Learning model to stay at. Apart from the solutions discussed earlier, we have used Spark/Flink, Apache Beam, and so on to deploy the model.

Once the model has been deployed in production, we now monitor the performance of the model on a real-world unseen dataset. We constantly gauge the performance. Now the model has entered the maintenance phase, wherein we have to ensure that the model is able to perform up to the mark and deliver results. In Figure 8-10, we are describing the model maintenance plan.

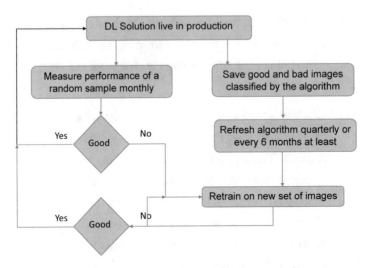

Figure 8-10. *Model maintenance is required to ensure that the model performs well in the long term and is able to meet the business requirements in delivering the output*

There are a few points which are crucial to note for model maintenance:

1. Once the solution is live and is used in making the predictions on the unseen dataset. But the performance of the algorithm is based on the training dataset which has been used to train the algorithm. There are going to be a few classes which are going to be unseen by the algorithm in the training phase. In other words, there can be a few classes which are underrepresented in the training data. The model might not perform well on those classes.

2. It is imperative that we monitor the performance at regular intervals. We might take a small sample of real-world images and grade those images manually. We can then compare with the actual prediction given by the model and check if the model is performing well. If the model's precision/recall has fallen below the threshold, it means the model requires refresh.

3. It is also vital to do a periodic refresh of the model. For example, once in 6 months or once in a year, it is recommended to retrain the model on a newer set of images.

4. Once the new version of the model is ready, we compare its performance to ensure that the new performance has improved. Only if the performance has improved, then we redeploy this new model in production.

5. For model refresh to be successful, we have to save the real-world unseen images for retraining purposes. A good strategy can be to save a small subset on a daily basis so that variation across phase and times can be captured. These images can be graded and used once we have to retrain the algorithm.

In this entire process, it is imperative that business stakeholders are an integral part of the discussion. Ultimately, they own the solution and are the primary stakeholders in it.

This concludes an end-to-end Deep Learning model development process. We can now move to the summary of the chapter.

8.9 Summary

Deep Learning is an evolving field. And so is computer vision. Computer vision using Deep Learning is one of the most sought-after solutions which are changing the entire landscape. They are much more sophisticated, innovative, concrete, and maintainable solutions. They are able to extend the capabilities by a much larger extent than other solutions. The usages are across all the domains – retail, telecom, aviation, BFSI, manufacturing, utilities, and so on.

The efficacy of the solution depends on a lot of factors like business problem definition, training data, hardware availability, accuracy KPI, and so on. Perhaps the most important component is the training data which is used to train the model. Getting concrete, complete, and representative training data is really a tedious task. And once this is achieved, a lot of ground is covered.

In this book, we have explored the various Neural Network architectures for computer vision problems. We started with the basics of computer vision and understood a few examples using OpenCV. Then we studied the basics of convolutional Neural Networks and their components in detail. From the third chapter onward, we started our journey with LeNet and further discussed a lot of architectures like VGG16, AlexNet, R-CNN, Fast R-CNN, Faster R-CNN, YOLO, SSD, DeepFace, and FaceNet. All these architectures are examined along with the actual Python implementations. We have developed use cases like binary image classification, multiclass image classification, object detection in a live video capture, face detection, gesture recognition, face identification, video analytics, image augmentation techniques, and so on. CNN and the various architectures have been helpful to develop them.

There are other branches of Neural Networks like recurrent Neural Networks, GAN, auto-encoders, and so on. Neural Networks are making an impact on not only the computer vision field but on natural language processing, audio analysis, and so on. There are quite a few novel usages like speech to text conversion, machine translation, summary generation, speech sentiment analysis, voice identification, and so on.

But this is not the end. There is still a very long way to go. You are advised to continue on this path to learn new concepts, explore ideas, and uncover novel technologies. At the same time, you should remember that artificial intelligence is a two-edged sword. It has to be used with caution. It should be used for uplifting the poor and oppressed, improving the medical facilities, and fighting hunger and injustice in the world. It can be used for destruction and violence too, but as responsible human beings, it is our responsibility to avoid using artificial intelligence for the wrong purpose.

With this, we close this chapter and the book. All the very best in your journey ahead!

You should be able to answer the questions in the exercise now! There are a few references at the end of the chapter. They give a quick refresher of the activation functions, Image Processing methods, various layers of Keras and their usage, and different types of image formats along with the respective differences in them.

REVIEW EXERCISES

You are advised to solve these questions:

1. What are the various steps in the model deployment process?

2. How can we tackle overfitting in the model?

3. Take a picture of your face and rotate it by 10 degrees using Python.

4. Use the image augmentation techniques in this chapter to improve the datasets in the previous chapters and compare the respective accuracies.

8.9.1 Further readings

1. Go through the research paper "Reducing the Training Time of Neural Networks by Partitioning": https://arxiv.org/abs/1511.02954.

2. Explore "Improve the Accuracy of Neural Networks using Capsule Layers": https://ieeexplore.ieee.org/document/8928194.

3. Go through the paper "Improving the Accuracy of Convolutional Neural Networks by Identifying and Removing Outlier Images in Datasets Using t-SNE": www.mdpi.com/2227-7390/8/5/662.

4. Explore "Active Bias: Training More Accurate Neural Networks by Emphasizing High Variance Samples": https://papers.nips.cc/paper/2017/file/2f37d10131f2a483a8dd005b3d14b0d9-Paper.pdf.

5. Read the paper "CSPNet: A New Backbone That Can Enhance Learning Capability of CNN": https://arxiv.org/pdf/1911.11929v1.pdf.

References

Major activation functions and layers used in CNN

The layers and the links are given here for quick reference. The links direct to the Keras official page at keras.io. All the layers can be examined at `https://keras.io/api/layers/`. We are discussing the major ones here:

- Input object: Instantiates a Keras tensor. Used for input

- Dense layer: Most common densely connected Neural Network layer

- Activation layer: Used to apply the activation functions

- Conv1D layer: 1D convolutional layer

- Conv2D layer: 2D convolutional layer

© Vaibhav Verdhan 2021
V. Verdhan, *Computer Vision Using Deep Learning*,
https://doi.org/10.1007/978-1-4842-6616-8

Name	Plot	Equation	Derivative
Identity		$f(x) = x$	$f'(x) = 1$
Binary step		$f(x) = \begin{cases} 0 & \text{for } x < 0 \\ 1 & \text{for } x \geq 0 \end{cases}$	$f'(x) = \begin{cases} 0 & \text{for } x \neq 0 \\ ? & \text{for } x = 0 \end{cases}$
Logistic (a. k. a Soft step)		$f(x) = \dfrac{1}{1 + e^{-x}}$	$f'(x) = f(x)(1 - f(x))$
TanH		$f(x) = \tanh(x) = \dfrac{2}{1 + e^{-2x}} - 1$	$f'(x) = 1 - f(x)^2$
ArcTan		$f(x) = \tan^{-1}(x)$	$f'(x) = \dfrac{1}{x^2 + 1}$
Rectified Linear Unit (ReLU)		$f(x) = \begin{cases} 0 & \text{for } x < 0 \\ x & \text{for } x \geq 0 \end{cases}$	$f'(x) = \begin{cases} 0 & \text{for } x < 0 \\ 1 & \text{for } x \geq 0 \end{cases}$
Parameteric Rectified Linear Unit (PReLU) [2]		$f(x) = \begin{cases} \alpha x & \text{for } x < 0 \\ x & \text{for } x \geq 0 \end{cases}$	$f'(x) = \begin{cases} \alpha & \text{for } x < 0 \\ 1 & \text{for } x \geq 0 \end{cases}$
Exponential Linear Unit (ELU) [3]		$f(x) = \begin{cases} \alpha(e^x - 1) & \text{for } x < 0 \\ x & \text{for } x \geq 0 \end{cases}$	$f'(x) = \begin{cases} f(x) + \alpha & \text{for } x < 0 \\ 1 & \text{for } x \geq 0 \end{cases}$
SoftPlus		$f(x) = \log_e(1 + e^x)$	$f'(x) = \dfrac{1}{1 + e^{-x}}$

Google Colab

Google Colab allows us to use the power of GPU for free. It is very easy to set up and use. Simply follow these nine steps.

Step 1: Go to your Google Drive and create a folder of choice.

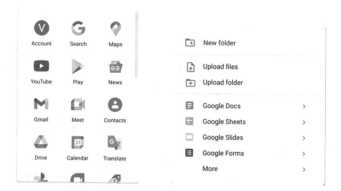

Step 2: Go to https://colab.research.google.com/. It will open a new window. You can select New notebook. Alternatively, you can cancel it and create a new notebook from the main page.

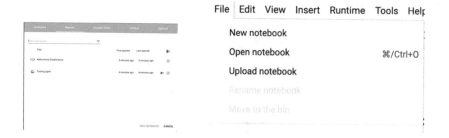

Step 3: In both the cases, you will get a new Jupyter Notebook.

Step 4: Rename it and you are good to use it like a regular Python Jupyter Notebook.

Step 5: You can link your Google Drive to it by using the following code:

The authorization code can be received by clicking the URL.

Step 6: Installation of any package is simple.

Step 7: You are good to use Google Colab. On the left side of the window, you can see the drives which are connected. You can go to any drive of your choice.

Step 8: To increase the computation speed, go to the runtime menu at the top, select Change Runtime type, and select GPU from the options.

Step 9: If you want to download the notebook, go to the File menu and download the Jupyter Notebook.

Index

© Vaibhav Verdhan 2021
V. Verdhan, *Computer Vision Using Deep Learning*,
https://doi.org/10.1007/978-1-4842-6616-8

Y, Z

Printed in the United States
By Bookmasters